Are you

Setting the Pace

...or taking up space?

You will either lead or be led or do absolutely nothing with your work life. This book will take you on an exploration of "you" and help you understand whether you fit into the equation of leadership.

By Peg Tobin, R.N.

Copyright © 2015 by Peg Tobin

All rights reserved. This book or any portion thereof may not be reproduced or used in any manner whatsoever without the express written permission of the publisher except for the use of brief quotations in a book review.

Printed in the United States of America

First Edition, 2015

ISBN-13: 978-1506131320

ISBN-10: 1506131328

Contact Information:

Peg Tobin

8233 Howe Industrial Parkway

Canal Winchester, OH 43110

www.tobinsearch.com

TABLE OF CONTENTS

ACKNOWLEDGEMENTS 4

INTRODUCTION 5

CHAPTER 1
    Take Off the Veneer, and Put Your Career in Gear 11

CHAPTER 2
    Motive Moves You, Fulfillment Keeps You 27

CHAPTER 3
    The Power Within Is the Power That Wins 39

CHAPTER 4
    Knowing the Terrain Helps You Stay on the Train 47

CHAPTER 5
    Perspective Is Relative 59

CHAPTER 6
    Cornerstone 71

CHAPTER 7
    Sand Traps 81

CHAPTER 8
    Which Hat Shall I Wear Today? 101

CHAPTER 9
    Change Starts with YOU! 119

CHAPTER 10
    My Roots Are Showing! 123

USEFUL TIPS
    Interviews & Resumes 138

ACKNOWLEDGEMENTS

To God, who makes all things possible in my life!

To my wonderful husband Richard, for being so supportive and encouraging throughout our lives together. Your acceptance and love make me feel like I can attempt anything and succeed.

To William Tobin, you are a blessing beyond words. Your support and love have given me the courage to step away from the company and do other things. This book is one of those "other things."

To Chris Tobin, thank you for keeping me connected to joy. You spark my imagination and encourage me to dream. This book became possible because you encouraged me to dream and put it down in writing.

To Darrell Donalds, thanks again for being able to reach into my mind to translate my thoughts and come up with just the right graphics.

To the Tobin Team, I don't know how our company, Tobin & Associates, would survive without your loyalty, professionalism and support. Thank you for making me "look" so good!

INTRODUCTION

As you go through life, you will be introduced to many individuals. If you are wise, you will take the opportunity to learn from each one who crosses your path.

A person destined to lead also knows how to follow. The difference between being the full-time follower and the leader temporarily following is that a leader will follow long enough to learn what to do, and then break away and set the pace for others to follow.

Without followers, a leader is just someone walking around talking and "taking up space." Followers are like the filling in the pie, which, as we all know, makes the pie worth eating. Followers are the brawn, brains and bodies that bring the leader's vision to life.

Like the leader without followers, you do not want to be an individual whose sole purpose in life is to take up space. You want to make a difference, either as a leader (setting the pace) or a follower (supporting the pace). "Space takers," unfortunately, exist only to exist! They live off of others and contribute nothing. They use our oxygen, pollute our earth and drain our energy. They think they are entitled to the rewards the rest of us work so hard to earn.

If you are not setting or supporting the pace, then you may be a space taker. If that's the case, this book is definitely not going to be your cup of tea.

This book is meant to help you explore various leadership styles and examine what influences a person to choose a particular leadership approach. The personalities and experiences in a person's life shape their strengths and create their reactions to situations; therefore, it is important for you to learn about and understand:

1. Yourself
2. How your past has developed your dominant characteristics
3. Why you react the way you do
4. Why you perceive things the way you do
5. Your strengths
6. Your hot buttons
7. Your doubts
8. Your dreams and desires
9. Your timing to step aside and move on to a new position
10. Your next adventure

There are many leadership styles:

- Transactional
- Autocratic
- Bureaucratic
- Charismatic
- Democratic/Participative
- Laissez-faire
- Task-oriented
- People/Relations-oriented
- Servant
- Transformational

It is true that one leadership style will dominate more than another in your life; but it is also true that a successful leader will use many leadership styles when dealing with multiple associates and peers. *The desired outcome may be similar but the approach may be different to obtain the optimal outcome.* Just as you would not approach a 14-year-old the same way you would approach a 20-year-old regarding a similar issue, a leader will not approach the majority of front-line associates the same way they approach a department director.

Take, for instance, a running back on a football team. When he gets the football, his objective is to take it all the way to the end zone and score a touchdown. However, you will notice that the "seas do not part" as in the Bible for Moses. Instead, this running back often has to deviate from a straight line and apply techniques such as jumping, twisting and dodging to avoid the obstacles that are trying to block him from his objective. This is the way it is with leadership. As leaders, we encounter obstacles that require us to be flexible in our approach as we pursue our objective.

Have you ever met someone who makes your skin crawl and you can't wait to get away from them? Alternately, have you ever met someone whom you can't get enough of? You are experiencing the cultural fit syndrome. Cultural fit is the reason an administrator may underperform for one organization yet excel for another. This is the very reason an organization should not judge an individual solely on their last employment. I have dealt with administrative personnel who performed wonderfully in their last position and brought a lot of ROI (return on investment) to the table but for some reason could not make this happen in their new environment. Cultural fits deal with a person's beliefs, morals and personality. When you mix two people who come from two totally different perspectives, success is hard to achieve. (Hint: It doesn't work for marriages either.)

When I was a kid, my granny taught me there is a God. She thanked Him for everything in her life and always told me God would take care of me. Therefore, when things did not appear to be working well for my family or me, I prayed to God. In my leadership adventures, I have turned to God many, many times. Therefore, for me to work for an organization that does not believe in God would probably not prove to be beneficial for the organization or for me. How would I ever shine in an organization that would not accept that I give all the praise to God for my accomplishments?

I received a lot of positive feedback from the readers of my first book, "Delegate or Suffocate," and I appreciated every comment. There isn't a person alive who doesn't want to know that the effort they put forth is worth it and that what they did meant something to someone. Thanks to each and every one of you who read my book. As I read your comments and met many of you, I realized from your questions there was more to cover and that I needed to write another book! Therefore, here we go again! You will find as you read that I have included some small portions of "Delegate or Suffocate," but only a few and only because they support the message I'm trying to relay to you in this book. This time around, my wish is for you to take a deeper look at yourself and learn what motivates you to make the decisions you do!

It is my belief that leaders can't truly lead until they understand what makes themselves tick. Leaders serve: They are put in their positions to make things happen through others. That means they need a heart to develop others and a desire to watch others succeed.

"A leader is best when people barely know he exists, when his work is done, his aim fulfilled, they will say: we did it ourselves."
—Lao Tzu

CHAPTER 1

Take Off the Veneer and Put Your Career in Gear

"What lies behind the mask delivers truth."

I know that, given my astonishingly good looks and superb figure, this is going to be tough to imagine, but *I did not sleep my way to the top!* There it is – now you know! Despite all the offers I received (well, really only one), I insisted that I *work* my way up to the corporate level.

I stood firm and fought off all one of the offers I received! No matter how tempting it was (*not*), I resisted. One day when I was in my first management position, I was in the med room by the nurses' station setting up a TPN solution. In walked the chief of surgery – all 5'1" of him! His balding head and robust 83-pound physique of well-defined muscles were hard to resist. He blocked my way out by standing in front of the only door, then quickly closed the door and began to share in his broken English how luscious he thought I was! I looked around to see if anyone else was there. *Oh, please, someone else be in this room!* Nope, it was just me. He came closer – so close I could tell he had eaten fish for lunch. He continued to ask me if I would like to have dinner with him. He said, "Perhaps if the meal goes well, we can extend the evening to my home for drinks and a swim in the pool. Do not worry about bringing a swimming suit."

Sure – my one chance for an affair and I get Don Knotts instead of Tom Selleck! I decided there was no job worth going to bed with the likes of this doctor, and I politely told him to bug off. I didn't use those exact words (although I did keep them clean), but he got the message.

Scientists say we are born with innate personalities and how we develop depends on the environment in which we grow. Therefore, I place complete blame on my parents for how I turned out. I could have been rich and famous very young if only they had inspired me appropriately. But – *oh no!* – I had to have hardworking parents who were satisfied with who they were and what they had!

As a young girl, I was gregarious and fidgety. In church, my mother would pinch me and tell me to be still. (Yeah, like that was going to help; instead, I just learned to sit out of her reach!) I didn't know what quiet was, and I certainly didn't know what it was like to sit and watch TV (part of that was because we didn't own a TV until I was 8). As I mentioned in my first book, I was a military child and that was the only life I knew. I was free to roam the entire base; therefore, I would leave the house in the morning on non-school days, carrying a peanut butter sandwich, and return in time for supper. Read a book, write a letter or play a board game? Not on my agenda! Running, jumping, skipping and other thoughtless activities filled my day.

At my high-school graduation rehearsal, I knew for sure the principal was going to come along and pull me out of line and tell me I had flunked. I never thought I would go to college; I just didn't think it was in the cards for me. I loved people, and I loved being involved with them. Having friends and enjoying them was what made my world go around. Therefore, I would have to agree that I was born with this personality trait. It remains with me today. No surprise when I take a personality test it reveals that I am a "people person" and that I should go for a career in public nursing or teaching. Imagine that neither opera singer nor movie star makes the list!

Life has taken many turns through the years, and even though I am still a fidgety person, I am no longer a young lady running through life skipping and jumping without a thought in my head. I eventually did go to college because I learned that fulfilling my passion necessitated my earning a degree to help open doors. Not only did I go to college, I went twice (and no, not because I flunked the first time!).

I have learned that dreams really can come true if you remain true to yourself and rely on your faith and your strengths to get you there. Like the child that wanted a puppy for Christmas and received a bag of poop, I believe that instead of crying, you should go on a quest to find the puppy that left the poop. Poop does happen, but if you look hard enough, you will find a cute puppy to make you happy (and a shovel to move the poop out of the way).

It is unfortunate that some people in this world seem to want to be miserable. No matter what you say to them, they refuse to become more positive. It may even feel like their life's goal is to make you as miserable as they are! My recommendation when you come across this type of person is to turn in the opposite direction and move as fast as you can away from them.

For a short time in my life, I could have easily gone down the path of misery. I tended to focus on the bad things in my life and talk about them – a *lot*. Fortunately for me, I got tired of hearing myself talk and I certainly got tired of the "poor me," hard life story. *Geez... hush up, Peg!*

I did have a challenging life, though. My dad was an alcoholic, and his addiction definitely caused pain for every member of our family. However, all of us who have faced misfortune can choose to wallow in our misery or pull ourselves up by our bootstraps and move on. **My past is my past. It is part of who I am today, but it does not totally define me.**

I went to a leadership workshop a few weeks back, and the first thing they had us do was take a personality test. At first I chuckled but, oddly enough, I found myself wanting to take the test and see my results. I think this action aligns with the personality trait in me that says I am curious. In my work career, I have taken several personality and strengths tests, and every time the results are the same. Therefore, you have to wonder why I was so eager to take another one. I have no sane answer.

At first I took these tests because I wanted to validate what I thought my strengths were, but now I do them for fun. Personality tests can become psychological gimmicks used to direct your way of thinking about yourself and classify you into a category. Please avoid classifying yourself. Use personality tests cautiously. I'm not against them; I just think they should be used only to show you your strengths and help you understand the personalities that reside in you as well as your staff. Tests like these should never be used to replace face-to-face interaction, and they should never be used as the sole reason to promote or hire a person. They should certainly *never* be used to *not* promote or hire a person.

Scientists have proven there are some common traits found in great leaders, but they have also found there are some great leaders with traits indicating they should never have succeeded in leadership. *Yet they did!* One of those leaders lacking strong leadership traits was King George VI. Despite this lack – and his stutter – King George VI ended up being extremely successful at reuniting the king with his people through his reign and involvement with World War II:

On VE (Victory in Europe) Day, 8 May 1945, Buckingham Palace was a focal point of the celebrations. The war had immeasurably strengthened the link between the King and his people. (The Official Website of The British Monarchy)

If you hold a leadership role, then something inside you brought you to this position. Don't let others tell you not to do it. Discover your strengths and build on them. I highly recommend that you do not get caught up in trying to strengthen your weaknesses; instead, spend your time surrounding yourself with individuals who have the strengths you lack. Build a team!

As I stated in "Delegate or Suffocate," Chapter 2 (Reality Bites!), page 30: ***Add to the team by hiring and promoting staff for their strengths and for what they bring to the table to address the needs of the unit.***

Surround yourself with those who can complement your strengths and carry your weaknesses. *This is called a team!* No one person can fill all positions. Analyze your strengths.

If you are:

- Social: hire someone quiet
- Quiet: hire someone social
- Analytical: hire a doer
- etc.

When I first started my leadership career, I thought that if I wanted to become outstanding, I needed to observe successful leaders and try to emulate their behavior. I did this as long as it took me to realize I was no longer in high school, and there was no way I could be a success by trying to be someone I was not. This doesn't mean that I stopped listening to what successful leaders had to say or tapping into the wisdom they had gained through their years of experience. Rather, I am just saying, "I've gotta be me!" – a freckle-faced, southern-speaking, sarcastic, huggie individual.

    Florence Littauer, a Christian self-help author and public speaker, developed a personality test called Personality Plus Profile. The test is simple to take and easy to understand. It has been proven over time to be a strong tool for revealing an individual's strengths. Her test is based on the four temperaments of Hippocrates, the "Father of Medical Science," who worked 350 years before the birth of Christ. Hippocrates used the predominant bodily fluids to explain the differences in human personalities.

Therefore, he classified personality traits as:

- Choleric
- Sanguine
- Phlegmatic
- Melancholic

*Go to quibblo.com/quiz/2FF0QY4/Personality-Plus-Test to access this Personality Plus Profile test.

    This test is not a deep and involved profile such as the StrengthsFinder Profile by the Gallup Company, but it will help you center in on your obvious strengths and get you started on developing yourself to be a top leader.

    When you take the test, you will find you possess a combination of all four classifications. Everyone has a piece that can be very outgoing and another that likes peace at all cost. The classification that scores the highest indicates your most natural behavior.

    I am going to cover these four classifications and add another classification at the end of each of Ms. Littauer's classifications. The additional classifications are from another personality test you may have heard of: the DiSC® Personality Test. You can take the test free at discpersonalitytesting.com.

After each breakdown and description, I will share my thoughts as to which positions may best serve the different personalities.

The DiSC Personality Profile is based on the work of renowned psychologist Dr. William Moulton Marston, and was introduced in his 1928 book "Emotions of Normal People." Dr. Marston developed the DiSC assessment as a tool to measure four primary behavioral traits:

Dominance (D)

Influence (i)

Steadiness (S)

Conscientiousness (C)

Dr. Marston never actually developed a DiSC Test or DiSC Assessment to measure these four DiSC styles. In 1940, Walter Clark took the theory of William Moulton Marston and developed the first DiSC Assessment.

A. Popular - Sanguine

According to Florence Littauer, a person whose dominant traits fall under the category of Sanguine is a charming person who attracts ... everyone!

This type of person is also likely to display these traits: being the center of attention, exuding energy, being talkative, having a good sense of humor, making friends very easily, being a favorite with friends as well as a great parent, and not holding grudges.

But Littauer also states that such a personality type tends to forget responsibilities and at times is egoistical and loud.

At work, Sanguine individuals are enthusiastic – always volunteering for new jobs, for example. They thrive on variety. They are capable and they keep co-workers motivated and happy.

They have a lot of energy, but they do struggle to keep their priorities in order.

DiSC Personality Test - Inducement: This type of person perceives him- or herself as more powerful than the environment, and perceives the environment as favorable.

Influence: People with high "i" scores influence others through talking and activity, and tend to be emotional. They are described as convincing, magnetic, political, enthusiastic, persuasive, warm, demonstrative, trusting and optimistic. Those with low "i" scores influence more through data and facts than through feelings. They are described as reflective, factual, calculating, skeptical, logical, suspicious, matter-of-fact, pessimistic and critical.

Sanguine traits might be beneficial to individuals in sales and marketing positions, activity coordinators, coaches, admission coordinators, educators, staff development professionals, etc.

B. Powerful - Choleric

Littauer's personality analysis test says that a Choleric individual is a very dynamic person.

This type of person is typically a born leader with great motivational skills who is cold-hearted, strong-willed and independent. The test says such individuals should be careful while dealing with others because they don't want to come across as arrogant and dominating; they need to relax and be less rigid. They should control their temper and learn to say "I'm sorry."

At work, Choleric individuals can see the bigger picture and plan goals carefully; they are good at delegating work and getting things organized.

However, they tend to use people and can be rude. They also tend to run their home like their office, with everything planned and organized.

DiSC Test - Dominance: Like a Sanguine, a Choleric person perceives him- or herself as more powerful than the environment;

however, the Choleric perceives the environment as unfavorable (as opposed to the Sanguine).

Drive: People who score high in the intensity of the "D" styles factor are very active in dealing with problems and challenges, while low "D" scores reflect people who want to do more research before committing to a decision. High "D" people are described as demanding, forceful, egocentric, strong-willed, driving, determined, ambitious, aggressive and pioneering. Low "D" scores describe those who are conservative, low-key, cooperative, calculating, undemanding, cautious, mild, agreeable, modest and peaceful.

Choleric traits might fit in with being an administrator, CEO, COO, chief nursing officer, manager, leader, owner, entrepreneur, regional manager, etc.

C. Perfect - Melancholy

A Personality Plus Test with Melancholy as the dominant trait is logical and has an analytical frame of mind.

Other traits include the following: serious by nature, always deep in thought, gifted with great creative and artistic skills, caring about others and always there in times of trouble. These individuals generally do not make good parents because their logical and analytical thinking has a tendency to make a child's life difficult. They prove to be a good and devoted friend who prefers to remain on the sidelines.

At work, Melancholy types are perfectionists who maintain high standards and are good with facts and figures – particularly small details. This type of person always finishes what he/she starts.

DiSC Test - Compliance: Perceives oneself as less powerful than the environment, and perceives the environment as unfavorable.

Compliance: People with high "C" styles adhere to rules, regulations and structure. They like to do high-quality work and do it right the first time. High "C" people are careful, cautious, exacting, neat, systematic, diplomatic, accurate and tactful. Those with low "C" scores challenge the rules and want independence. They might be described as self-willed, stubborn, opinionated, unsystematic, arbitrary and unconcerned with details.

Melancholy traits might be beneficial to a CFO, compliance director, accountant, human resources representative, inspector, records keeper, department manager, etc.

D. Peaceful - Phlegmatic

People with Phlegmatic as their dominant trait are cool and calm. Other traits are: not easily flustered, taking problems in stride, patient and usually kind, reliable and consistent. Phlegmatic types are patient with children and share a good friendly rapport with them. Others enjoy their company because of their amicable and pleasant nature. They tend to be shy and remain in the background. They need to be responsible for their own actions and learn to adapt to changes.

At work, they can tend to be casual, lazy and careless, but they get along well with one and all, they are good at administrative jobs, solving problems and mediating between people.

DiSC Test - Submission: Perceives oneself as less powerful than the environment, and perceives the environment as favorable.

Steadiness: People with high "S" scores want security and a steady pace, and do not like sudden change. High "S" individuals are calm, relaxed, patient, possessive, predictable, deliberate, stable and consistent. They tend to be unemotional and poker-faced. Low "S" intensity scores are those who like change and variety. People with low "S" scores are described as restless, demonstrative, impatient, eager and even impulsive.

Phlegmatic traits might fit in with being a dietitian, social worker, assistant manager, assistant pastor, writer, nun, teacher, volunteer, quiet leader, support team member, caregiver, etc.

"Leaders think and talk about the solutions. Followers think and talk about the problems." —Brian Tracy

Considering this definition of "strength" – an action you see yourself doing over and over again and doing with joy – you probably could find your own strengths without taking a test. However, if you want to go the route of observation, then try doing and answering the following:

Observe how you respond when you are put in a situation that requires an emergent action. What is programmed into you from your strengths and talents will show up in your first response.

1. When you are at a social gathering, are you drawn to speak with people you don't know? Or do you stick close to those you know?
2. When given the opportunity to go out and be social or stay at home with close friends, which would you rather do?
3. How do you act when an associate calls off from work because they have a sick child?
4. What is your first instinct when you find an associate has been manipulating situations to make him- or herself look good?
5. Do you delay answering a question until you have all the details? Or do you give an answer based on the information you have at your disposal at that given time?
6. When you have another challenge put on your desk, how do you react?
7. After you achieve a goal, what do you do?
8. When faced with complex situations with multiple variables, how do you respond? Once you form an opinion, what do you do with it?
9. When you are sharing an idea, do you share it in parables, metaphors, etc.? Or do you get right to the point?
10. When you lose in a competition, how do you conduct yourself?

11. How do you function outside of order?
12. Do you treat all employees the same?
13. Where do you go for direction?
14. When you are walking around at work, what types of things do you relay to your associates?
15. When you go out to eat with your staff, do you want to pay for everyone?
16. What kind of activities make you want to participate?
17. What kind of activities make you want to tune out and avoid?
18. What is a recurring pattern of behavior in you (such as being instinctively inquisitive, competitive, charming, persistent, responsible, communicative, empathetic, strategic, open-minded, etc.)?
19. What can you do as well as the best leaders you know?
20. What is the most common driving motive behind your actions?
21. What do you hope co-workers will say are your greatest strengths?
22. Considering the achievement of which you are most proud, which of your strengths do you think helped you succeed?

    If you are the type of person who will step up and step into a challenge, then you are likely a Choleric. If there is a crisis going on, then you are the person to lead the team and bring on others to balance out what the organization needs.

    If you like order and don't like to move on to another project until you have completed the one you are currently working on, then you are likely a Melancholy. When a unit or department needs to be organized, they will want you on their team. You think before you act.

If you care about those around you and like to bring joy into others' lives, then you are likely a Sanguine. Sanguines bring happiness and fun to a team. They are needed to lighten the mood and give the team optimism.

If you are quiet and you like peace at any cost, then you are likely a Phlegmatic. Phlegmatics bring harmony to a team. They are slow to answer, but once they make up their minds, they stand firm and do not waiver.

Every one of these personalities can be a leader. ***The need of the whole dictates the leader you will ask to step up to the plate.*** A team wins together. No one person is better or more important than another. If you are outgoing, kind and affectionate, then you need to be looking for the take-charge person who is going to organize the plan of action.

Now you are the body of Christ, and each one of you is a part of it. —1 Corinthians 12 v 27

If your career is not flowing, **then stop and take your sunglasses off and see who you are behind the veneer you have put on.** Find out why you think you have to act the way you do. If you are not being totally you, then what message are you sending to your staff?

I worked with a regional director in the organization where I held a parallel position. Fortunately, we worked in different regions. This regional director thought everyone should do everything the way she did it. She came in with a stomp and demanded everyone learn to think like her and handle all situations as she would. I was asked by the company to go with her to a few of her facilities and assist her with a few reimbursement issues. After one week with this lady, I returned to my region thanking God that I didn't have to answer to an individual like her. Being the person I am, I did ask her why she insisted everyone do everything her way. She turned to me and snidely stated, "Because I am right and they are not." This individual was quick to say that if I worked for her, she would fire me!

As Paul Harvey would say, "the rest of the story":

A year later, this individual was charged with falsifying her records to qualify for a position. She lost her opportunity to enhance her career and the license she did possess was put on review.

You would think incidents like this would make a person humble, but not this person. I saw her a few years later at a convention. I went over to say hello and ask her how she was doing. She looked at me and said, "What business is it of yours?" I turned and said, "You're right, it is not my business and I don't care!" I walked away and haven't seen her since.

"Outstanding leaders go out of their way to boost the self-esteem of their personnel. If people believe in themselves, it's amazing what they can accomplish." —Sam Walton

CHAPTER 2

**Motive Moves You,
Fulfillment Keeps You**

"Wisdom clarifies vision."

Do you enter a conversation...

- To be heard?
- To be understood?
- To understand?

There are individuals who go into a conversation just for the opportunity to express themselves. They don't listen or care what the other individual in the conversation has to say. They don't even care what the conversation is about. They just talk to hear themselves speak. Usually these individuals speak loudly and don't adjust their volume or try to be sensitive to their surroundings.

Other individuals go into a conversation to be understood. These conversations tend to be confrontational because the ones wanting to be understood are pushing their opinions and thoughts onto the other people. They aren't interested in others' opinions or views. Their voices tend to grow louder as the conversation continues. These individuals are not sensitive to their surroundings either.

Individuals who go into a conversation to understand tend to talk less and listen more. Don't mistake their quiet and polite manner as resignation. These individuals join a conversation with the direct purpose of gaining knowledge. They aren't there to waste time or argue. However, these types of individuals have been known to push the "hot buttons" of the individuals who come to be understood. These individuals are very aware of their surroundings, and they know when to end conversations that are going nowhere.

If you go to a buffet-style luncheon, you will notice similar behavior in the three types of conversationalists as they go through the line:

- Mr./Ms. "to be heard" is usually first in line. They pile their plate high, making sure their needs are met. They usually don't look to see who is in line behind them or before them; their focus is on the food and getting enough for themself.

- Mr./Ms. "to be understood" takes authority of the line and comments on the food as they go through the line, usually questioning the reason for serving this kind of food. However, they do not shy away from taking enough to satisfy their hunger.
- Mr./Ms. "to understand" takes their time getting to the line. They tend to linger back and let others go in front of them. Their conversations and comments as they go through the line are focused on the individuals surrounding them. They take what is left and continue to focus on positive conversations.

The trends that connect these individuals' behaviors in their conversations and buffet lines show up in just about any situation you put them in. That is because these are the personality traits that direct their lives.

Many companies/organizations are evaluating potential hires for their personality traits because time has shown that certain traits predispose an individual to being a successful leader.

The number one tool being used to do this assessment is called the Emotional Intelligence Theory, a theory developed by Daniel Goleman, which first appeared on the scene in 1995.

"The work of Daniel Goleman in developing his Emotional Intelligence theory has shown that while the IQ does not show to correlate well with leadership effectiveness, the EI does show a continuous positive correlation with effective leadership." (Tsnousis, 2003)

The difference in Intelligence Quotient (IQ) and Emotional Intelligence (EI) is this: Your IQ (your ability to learn) is the same at age 5 as it is at age 50; however, your EI (acquired skills) can improve with time and practice. A trait or skill to interact with others can be learned and improved upon with concentrated effort and work. However, the individual must be willing to recognize the need for the change and desire to do it. Therefore:

Leaders can be developed as well as born.

The higher a person's EI score, the greater their chance of being a successful leader! A high IQ score does not necessarily indicate a person will be a successful leader. Therefore:

People of ordinary or moderate intelligence can be great leaders.

In my experience, I have found that if a person lacks common sense, 99 percent of the time, they will not be a great leader.

"The difference between genius and stupidity is that genius has its limits." —Albert Einstein

According to Goleman's theory, the EI has four components:

Self-awareness

- Emotional self-awareness
- Accurate self-assessment
- Self-confidence

Self-management

- Self-control
- Trustworthiness
- Conscientiousness
- Adaptability
- Achievement orientation
- Initiative

The above two components deal with your ability to accurately perceive your emotions and stay aware of them. With awareness, you can manage your behavior and tendencies while positively redirecting your behavior.

The person who wanted "to be heard" had no emotions invested in the conversation and, therefore, was not engaged. The person who wanted "to be understood" let their emotions guide the whole conversation. "To understand" set their emotions aside and engaged in the conversation.

In other words: ***Great leaders learn to keep their emotions in their hip pocket and stay focused on the situation at hand.***

Social Awareness

- Empathy
- Organizational awareness
- Service orientation

Social Skills

- Visionary leadership
- Influence
- Developing others
- Communication
- Change catalyst
- Conflict management
- Building bonds
- Teamwork and collaboration

These components deal with your social awareness and relationship management skills. They predict your ability to understand other people's moods, behaviors and motives, which then will lead you to understand what is really going on and manage your interactions with others successfully.

If you care about those around you and reflect your concern back to them, acknowledging that life can get in the way of progress, then you will be able to help everyone find a way around the issues.

Daniel Goleman's theories are about relationships. If you know how to build a relationship, then you will know how to build a team.

"You can close more business in two months by becoming interested in other people than you can in two years by trying to get people interested in you." —Dale Carnegie

Mr. Goleman's studies gave credence to ideas that have been around for a long time. He put them in a format that is more understandable for this generation.

The following is a list I found on Wikipedia of individuals who should have never achieved success according to United States standards:

David Green, billionaire founder of Hobby Lobby, started the Hobby Lobby chain with only $600 and a high school diploma.

Andrew Carnegie, industrialist and philanthropist, and one of the first mega-billionaires in the United States, was an elementary school dropout.

Anne Beiler, multi-millionaire co-founder of Auntie Anne's Pretzels, did not complete high school.

Ashley Qualls, founder of Whateverlife.com, left high school to build her website business. She earned more than a million dollars by the time she was 17.

Barbara Lynch, chef and owner of a group of Boston restaurants worth over $10 million, dropped out of high school.

Bob Proctor, motivational speaker, bestselling author and co-founder of Life Success Publishing, attended only two months of high school.

Charles Culpeper, owner and CEO of Coca-Cola, dropped out of high school.

These individuals believed in themselves and tenaciously believed they could make things better. So in spite of U.S. standards or expectations, they became very successful.

It is written that none of these leaders started out with "top of mind" to make money; they started with "top of mind" to make a difference. Money was a by-product of their passion. You may not become a millionaire doing what you love, but you will love working at what you are doing.

"When nothing seems to help, I go and look at a stonecutter hammering away at his rock perhaps a hundred times without as much as a crack showing in it. Yet at the hundred and first blow, it will split in two, and I know it was not that blow that did it, but all that had gone before." —Jacob August Riis

If you are wondering if you are doing what you love, then ask yourself the following three questions:

1. What kind of work gets you excited to go to work every day?
2. Would *you* pay someone to do the kind of work you love?
3. What would you do if you were a millionaire?

Your answer to 1 and 3 should be the same and 2 should be a yes. If your answers don't line up, then you need to continue on to three more questions:

1. Do you know if anyone gets paid to do what you love to do?
2. How can you get the kind of job that makes you excited?
3. What is getting in your way of pursuing what you love?

If your answer to number 1 is no, then you are going to have to create a need for what you want to do, which means you will have to consider becoming an entrepreneur.

If you cannot answer number 2 quickly off the top of your head, then you may need to research your dream job.

If your answer to number 3 is "fear of failure" or "I just can't fit it into my schedule," then you may need to reexamine what you classify as a passion. If it is a true passion, you will see that it has been in you since you were a child and you have been burning to do it your whole life. Nothing should be getting in your way. Are you making your dream/passion a reality or a regret?

Fear exists only in your mind and has ground only when you give it recognition.

If there are organizations that offer your dream job, then:

- Find out what qualifications you need to get the position.
- If you have to gain qualifications, then set target dates to attain those qualifications.
- Contact the companies or departments you want to target. Show them your interest ahead of time.
- Write goal dates as to when you will contact each organization.
- Set clear objectives with timescales.
- Reach success.

Recognize and reward yourself every day for the steps you take toward attaining your passion.

If you are in a job you love, but you are not as happy as you think you should be and are not moving toward success, then ponder your motives:

- Did you accept the position for the opportunity to grow?
- Did you go for pay and benefits?
- Did you go to be you?
- Did you go to become a carbon copy of the leaders they already have?
- Did you go to develop others?
- Did you go to advance your career?

Dig deeper:
- Why did you accept the leadership role?
- Did you receive a "strengths and personality" test?
- Were you assigned a mentor?
- What did you hope to gain through your acceptance of the leadership role?

The following is a story shared by the great motivational speaker Zig Ziglar in one of his speeches:

In the 1950s, an incident took place on a sweltering summer afternoon alongside a railroad track where a crew of workers was doing some repair work. A train came chugging down the track and pulled off on a side rail. A window opened and a voice—a man's voice—shouted out, "Dave! Dave Anderson, is that you?"

It was; in fact, Dave Anderson was in charge of the crew. "Yeah, Jim, it's me," he shouted back.

The man on the train, Jim Murphy, yelled out, "Well, come on over here and let's chat a while."

So Dave stopped what he'd been doing and joined Jim Murphy in his private air-conditioned railroad car for almost an hour, no doubt happy to get out of the broiling sun. When the conversation ended, he made his way back to his crew working on the track. The flabbergasted crew stared at him in utter shock and said something to the effect of, "That was Jim Murphy, the president of the railroad."

"Yup, it sure was," Anderson said.

They all gathered around and excitedly wanted to know how Dave knew Jim Murphy, the president of the railroad, for God's sake, to say nothing about how he got to be such good buddies with the man and on a first-name basis to boot!

Dave explained: "Well, it's quite simple—when I started with the railroad over 20 years ago, Jim Murphy started at the same time; we've been pals ever since."

Now the crew is astonished as much as they are confused. They wanted to know how it is that Dave and Jim Murphy started working for the railroad at the same time and Murphy rose to such dizzying heights while old Dave is still working on the track in the hot sun. How in God's name did that happen?

Dave looked wistfully up into the sky and said, "A little over 20 years ago, Jim Murphy went to work for the railroad; I went to work for $1.75 an hour."

The attitude you take to your position will come from your motive, and if your motive is healthy for you then happiness and success will follow.

There is a definitive distinction between good, evil and bad leaders. Adolph Hitler had many followers, which undoubtedly made him a successful leader, but his driving motives were far different from Abraham Lincoln's.

"Whatever you are, be a good one." —Abraham Lincoln

CHAPTER 3

The Power Within Is the Power That Wins

"The least traveled path blossoms longer."

The words and behavior you have been raised with will have more to do with the development of your abilities and personality than any innate qualities that were instilled in you at conception through DNA.

The following is from Kathryn Stockett's book *"The Help"*:

All my life I'd been told what to believe about politics, coloreds, being a girl. But with Constantine's thumb pressed in my hand, **I realized I actually had a choice in what I could believe.**

This book and movie did an astonishing job of demonstrating what years of thinking, speaking and acting can do to future generations to form their beliefs regarding race, politics, gender and other biases. *If just one person who is important to you in your mind has negative thoughts about you and relays those thoughts to you, those spoken words will affect you immensely for as long as you give them credence.* **What you allow to enter your thoughts regarding your abilities will take seed and harvest in your actions.**

My mama was a beautician by trade but my dad did not approve of her working, so she stayed home and cared for her children and her husband. Our home life revolved around my father. Therefore, it was not surprising that I thought this was the path in life that I was supposed to take. My mama was content with her life; she loved her coffee klatches, where the ladies in the neighborhood would gather and discuss "the happenings" of "As the World Turns" and other daytime soap operas. To me, the thought of having to fill my day with such activities left me empty. But based on my upbringing, I didn't think I had a choice.

That was until a small crisis occurred in my family that threw me into a situation where I had to get a job fast to support my mother and myself. This crisis, which at first was viewed as bad, ended up to be one of the most wonderful gifts ever given to me. This occurrence:

1. Showed me that even though I had never held a job before, I impressed the interviewers well enough to hire me.

2. Proved to me that even though I thought I was *not* smart, I passed a math and English test with scores high enough to be offered a job immediately.
3. Demonstrated to me that I could provide a living for myself and not be dependent on a parent or future husband.

This crisis taught me independence. It was a huge turning point in my life.

I can't say that I remember ever being told I wasn't smart, but it was the opinion I formed about myself based on the fact that my school grades were usually low, and I had no one in my life telling me different. Far be it for me to think that perhaps my low grades might be attributed to the fact I attended 10 different schools in my 12 years of education, and that my dad's addiction caused us to have a turbulent home life. No, not me! Why would I think positive? Positive was not my family's traditional response. Therefore, I went down the path laid out in front of me and judged myself dumb. Poor, poor me, the victim – and dumb!

Getting this job and gaining independence gave me the hope to dream. I began to consider possibilities that my life's path was not laid out in front of me and perhaps I could be something different than my mother. Don't get me wrong: I loved my mama; I just didn't want to *be* her. I also loved my dad, but I certainly didn't want to be him. My dreams became a strong driver for me.

The next great environmental impact on my life came when I met and married Richard Tobin. He saw intelligence and beauty in me, and he reflected it back to me often. I began to dream even bigger, and with his support and our mutual faith in God, I started to believe I could accomplish some of my dreams.

"Know thyself means this, that you are acquainted with what you know, and what you can do." —Menander

If you want to be a leader, then be a leader. The fact that you have the desire and that you have walked through the door of opportunity are evidence that you have the right attitude to make it happen.

You can take lots of personality tests, but in time you will find your behavior and attitude are the keys to your strengths, and your belief in yourself is the driver that will bring you to success in leadership.

You are the only one who can control your *attitude*. You are also the one who controls your environment.

Definition of "attitude" (BusinessDictionary.com):

Attitude is a predisposition or a tendency to respond positively or negatively toward a certain idea, object, person or situation.

Attitude influences an individual's choice of action and responses to challenges, incentives and rewards (together called stimuli).

If you don't have a positive attitude about yourself, and if you don't trust your abilities, then your thoughts will be the noose around your neck that will kill your future. If you are in an environment that does not facilitate and contribute toward your growth, then you are doomed to routine. A positive attitude and encouraging environment are a must to success.

I put the following in "Delegate of Suffocate"; I am including it again because it is a good idea to assess if you have a winning and tenacious attitude. About leadership, R. E. Thompson wrote:

1. Do you welcome responsibility?
2. Do other people's failures annoy you or challenge you?
3. Do you use people or cultivate them?
4. Do you direct people or develop them?
5. Do you criticize or encourage?
6. Do you shun the problem person or seek them out?
7. Do you nurse resentments or readily forgive injuries done to you?

8. Are you reasonably optimistic?
9. Do you possess tact? Can you anticipate the likely effect of a statement before you make it?
10. Do your subordinates appear at ease in your presence?
11. Are you unduly dependent on the praise or approval of others?
12. Do you find it easy to make and keep friends?
13. Can you induce people to do happily some legitimate thing that they would not normally want to do?
14. Can you accept opposition to your viewpoint or decision without considering it a personal affront and reacting accordingly?
15. Are you entrusted with the handling of difficult and delicate situations?
16. Do you possess the ability to secure discipline without having to resort to a show of authority?
17. Do you readily secure the cooperation and win the respect and confidence of others?
18. Can you use disappointments creatively?
19. Can you handle criticism objectively and remain unmoved under it?
20. Do you retain control of yourself when things go wrong?

A positive attitude is a strength that will enable you:
- To set high goals, because you envision yourself achieving those goals
- To develop others beyond their highest expectations because you are able to reflect a positive image to them
- To take risks because you believe all things are possible

- To view obstacles as bumps in the road that will be removed with time and persistence

The strength of a positive attitude opens the doors to make success happen! Grab hold of your positive attitude and climb aboard the leadership train.

"Great leaders are not defined by the absence of weakness, but rather by the presence of clear strengths." —John Zenger

A person with a positive attitude will see things that are unseen to others. The following is a true story:

Above All

Ticket in hand, hair slicked back, large smile, blue eyes aglow, suitcase packed, tennis shoes tied, and shirt tucked into his pants, Christopher was ready to fly. However, this time there would be no stretching out his arms and running around the yard making noises like an airplane. Four-year-old Christopher was going for his very first airline ride.

"Mommy, look, look!" quickly replaced "Mommy, can we go?"

Christopher was already airborne as we entered the airport. He scampered ahead with a version of "touch and go" with every leap. Keeping up with Christopher meant never having to go to aerobics class. He raced into the cabin, eager to fly. His older brother at the window seat in front of him and his dad beside his brother, I strapped Christopher to his window seat and sat down beside him. The rest of the passengers boarded, and my little man chatted with anyone within range of his smile. When the flight attendant gave her safety speech, Christopher was as attentive as the RCA dog.

Soon we were in the air. While some passengers napped or read, Christopher got on his knees and pressed his face into the glass window. I guessed that he wanted to experience flying as "up-close and personal" as possible.

"Mommy, are we above the clouds?" Christopher asked.

I gazed out the window and said, "Yes, Christopher, we are."

He turned away from me and back to the window, peering this way and then that way. With a puzzled look on his face, he looked back at me and in his ever familiar quaking "boomlet" voice said, "Well, then, where's God?"

The cabin quickly filled with laughter, but just as quickly went silent, as each one of us searched within for the answer. You could hear a pin drop as the passengers leaned closer, the answer...

CHAPTER 4

Knowing the Terrain
Helps You Stay on the Train

"A thoroughbred requires no bridal."

Can you please hold the flashlight closer?
It's getting hard to see the light at the end of the tunnel!

HIMMS, MDS 3, OSHA, HCAHPS, Re-hospitalization Penalties, ACOs, Affordable Care Act, HIPAA, JCAHO, QIS, PPS, Quality Incentives, Satisfaction Surveys, 5 Star, etc., etc., etc.!

I am certain it is the same for all managers, but I know for nurse managers, every time they turn around, they are expected to adhere to new or perceived new compliances. The government sets deadlines, and it is up to you as the leader to ensure compliance or else your unit/facility will be monetarily fined by the regulatory agency.

Surveyors may not know what they are inspecting, but the nurse leader is required by law to have the new rules in place before the surveyors arrive. *Wow, and they wonder why nurses don't flock to be managers/leaders?*

Undoubtedly however, managers/leaders cannot complain about the alluring perks that come with their leadership position. *These perks are just too hard to resist:*

- You are able to lose weight easier, because you never get time to sit long enough to eat a meal.
- You never have to worry again about "bed head," because your head rarely hits the pillow long before you receive a call.
- The money you save on home utilities is phenomenal because you are never there!
- Toilet paper usage is reduced gravely because you only have time to go once a day.
- No worry about obtaining a cell phone or pager: The facility is sooooo... very nice and provides you with one.
- If you are on a challenged unit, you are spared the energy of developing relationships with staff, because the employees come and go using a revolving door.

- The spring in your step improves because you learn how to leap tall bedside commodes with a single bound and save a patient/resident from slipping to the floor.

- Your brain agility improves each day through your multitasking. You learn how to perform a bed bath, resolve scheduling issues, handle a physician's complaint and page housekeeping to clean up vomit, all at the same time. You are unstoppable.

- Where else could you work and also learn how to proficiently fill other professional positions as you hold down your own full-time position? You will become affluent in scheduling, cooking, housekeeping, admissions, social working, maintenance and more. The best thing about all this new training is that it is provided to you for free.

- The best perk of all is something they call "comp time." I'm not sure you will truly understand it, because when you ask for more detail, you are told they will get to you later. I'm still waiting, but I'm sure you will get an answer sooner than I. I'm not worried and I'm still excited, because I know somewhere out there I have a whole bunch of this "comp time" to cash in on when I get older.

You have to admit: With these great perks, it's hard to say no to the idea of being a manager or leader.

Maybe I'm slightly nuts, but no matter how hard the leadership positions have been at times, I am thankful for each and every one of those days of learning. Staff came and went, but each one of them tried to help make a difference.

There were times I remember interviewing people and thinking, "They are breathing, they can bend, they are certified. I wonder if they can start in 15 minutes?" Yes, it has been hard and it will be hard again, but no one can ignore the bottom line: Patients and residents need us.

There is a light at the end of the tunnel. No matter how dim it may appear at times, it does get brighter. With practice, all things get easier. As leaders, we have to learn how to survive because the sick and infirmed are not going to go away. **We are leaders because we love what we do and we bring to the table a passion that will not be satisfied by sitting on the sidelines.**

"The challenge of leadership is to be strong, but not rude; be kind, but not weak; be bold, but not bully; be thoughtful, but not lazy; be humble, but not timid; be proud, but not arrogant; have humor, but without folly." —Jim Rohn

Complaining has never really solved a problem. The squeaky wheel does get the oil, but that doesn't mean this is the right approach. Solutions and a desire to make things right solve problems! *I can complain about the fact I can no longer fit into a size 8, but if I really want to make it happen, I have to change my attitude and behavior.*

There are some things I will never change. It is inevitable I will grow older with each year until I die. There are also things about healthcare that I will never be able to change by myself. **Learning the difference between what is inevitable and what is changeable is a beginning toward a solution.**

Alone, can one person make a difference? At first you might be inclined to say no, but the truth is *yes!* You start with one voice, but with each voice added, *hope* gets louder. You have heard the phrase "Two heads are better than one"; can you imagine what a thousand voices could do?

Have you sat in an airport or a mall, watching people interact and trying to figure out who is leading, who is following, who is demanding, who is submissive, who is capable of tuning everyone out and continuing on their own path, who is sensitive and pouts, who is the social butterfly and who is the uptight organizer? *You have? Me, too!* If you can do that, then you can apply those same observational powers and figure out which personalities you have and need on your team, and start to make a difference.

It is highly unlikely that you are going to have all Cholerics or Sanguines in your department. God help you if you have all Melancholies; however, your unit will have a procedure for everything down to "how to burp appropriately." I may be exaggerating a little regarding the Melancholy. The best assistant I ever had was a Melancholy. She drove me crazy with her questions, but I knew I could relax and walk away and count on her to handle the details.

Hot buttons are buttons that people use to stretch you. When those buttons are pushed, nine times out of 10 you are upset because you are being asked to do something you don't like to do but know you have to do, and the child inside you is coming out and saying, "I don't want to eat my vegetables!"

It isn't wrong to dislike doing certain duties or chores; nevertheless, disliking doing something does not mean it will go away if you ignore it.

You cannot be rude to the person who is pushing your buttons, because they are just doing what comes natural to them. I knew my hot buttons long before I ever got my first management position. My sister definitely knew them, too. Since I was a mover and I liked to get things done so I could go out with my friends, my sister would inevitably go to the bathroom after supper each evening and sit in there a very long time. She knew if she dilly-dallied long enough, I would have finished the dishes and cleaned up the kitchen, and she wouldn't have to do anything.

One of my biggest hot buttons is to have someone sit and hash over the what-ifs with me. Listening to the what-ifs defeats me; I always feel like I'm being told "I cannot do it. It is not going to work."

I like to skim over contracts and make an educated judgment quickly as to whether I think the contract is advantageous for us or not. However, my eldest son (our CEO) reads and rereads every single solitary word in every single contract. Then he insists I sit with him and go over all the what-ifs. I smile and listen, but it drives me bananas. I know what he is doing, and it is important. I also know he is better at this than I am, and I am comfortable knowing he will know what is good for the company – that's why I delegated this responsibility to him. Fortunately for me, I have gotten him down to discussing only a few what-ifs at a time, and we both are much happier campers.

I am a people person and a strong leader, but believe it or not, I do know how to step back and be led. I like to learn from other experts, and it's fun to work with others who know how to acknowledge your qualities and appreciate what you bring to the table. I join committees just to learn from others.

If you pay attention to your hot buttons, they will let you know what kind of individuals you need on your team. Before William joined our company, I had to read all the contracts. I didn't like to do it, but I knew it had to be done – and done thoroughly – to protect the company. What a blessing it was when he decided to come to work with us! Our current core team has been together for nearly a decade now, and we definitely complement one another's strengths. It took us a while to get the right mix, but we did. Our director of Interim Services stated when we were going through some changes, "Yep, Peg turned the building upside down, but I dug my fingernails in and hung on." When you have a good teammate, they don't let go and you don't let go of them.

There are many styles of management, but the one I deem the most difficult to grow under is that of a micromanager. Micromanagers create boundaries that provide opportunities only for themselves to be rewarded, thus stunting others on the team.

Micromanagers tend to be insecure. They go overboard with everything because they want every i dotted and every t crossed to *protect themselves but not the whole team*. What makes a micromanager insecure may be immaterial, but the fact that they are is extremely important, because their insecure actions gravely affect everyone who works with them.

Micromanagers like to flex their muscles, controlling and manipulating others. They routinely dictate priorities and assign unreasonable deadlines. They want everything done their way and dismiss the very thought that anyone could have a better idea than them. They protect themselves by making their subordinates do a stream of needless reports.

> If a micromanager thinks something is wrong with the spaghetti being served, they will have the staff syphon off the sauce to get to the noodles. Then they will have you place the sauce in a pan for later. Once the noodles are exposed, they will have staff take every noodle, straighten them out, wash them, dry them, and examine them thoroughly. Then the staff will have to turn their attention to the sauce. They will be required to examine every ingredient identified and document their findings. If nothing is found, the micromanager will question the staff as to why **they** felt the need to go to such lengths for no apparent reason. However, if something is discovered, the micromanager will **gladly** take credit for the pain taking efforts and protective results.

Micromanagers are afraid that something is always going to go wrong and, of course, it will never be their fault. And because they think things will go wrong ... often things *do* go wrong. ***A person gets what they expect!***

These types of leaders have problems with trust and transparency. They believe they have to require everyone to go above and beyond the norm. Micromanagers insist that they themselves be involved in every aspect of every position, and they require decisions be personally approved by them. Therefore, problems do not get resolved efficiently. Unless this leader is a family member or owed a lifelong favor, they will eventually be replaced. In time, the leaders over the micromanager will identify the fact that the constant with the poor production in the micromanager's department is the manager.

In a weird way, micromanagers become self-fulfilling prophesiers. They are so worried something is going to go wrong and they are going to be fired that they can't relax. Their non-trusting actions produce more problems and fewer positive results, and eventually they are fired. The challenge is this: Until the micromanager is fired, how does one work with such an individual? I wish I could give you an easy, three-sentence answer; but I cannot. The bottom line is that it's very difficult to operate and grow under a micromanager.

However, I recommend these actions:

- Staff members should work together to support one another. If the staff members talk and recognize their leader struggles with trust, it will help ease the pain of a public tongue-lashing that the manager may give to exert their power and authority.

- Take copious notes when the micromanager is giving out directions, and then email a thank-you to the manager for taking the time to help everyone understand the objective. Include your notes of their directives in the email (you are creating a paper trail).

- Design tools and forms that can be used to inform the manager on the progress of every assignment (another paper trail).

- Do not deviate from the manager's rules. Be on time and prepared for every meeting.

- Anticipate and be prepared with numbers and percentages that are commonly asked for by the manager.

- Identify the staff member who best communicates with the manager and use that person to develop a relationship with the manager. Perhaps the staff member will help the manager resolve their insecurities.

- If you can move to another unit or facility, then do it.

- Role-play with one another to prepare yourselves to respond better in pressured times with the manager.

- Get together with your co-workers and bounce around ideas that you can apply to solve the issues.

- Pray that the micromanager finds peace and is able to trust in others.

If you get to the point where you can't take it any longer, before you quit, take the time to have a tough conversation with your manager! You will risk your comfort, but with today's rules regarding retribution toward an employee, you should be protected. The one thing I can tell you with assurance is this: **If you say nothing, nothing will change.**

"No man will make a great leader who wants to do it all himself, or to get all the credit for doing it." —Andrew Carnegie

Wisdom takes root when you learn the best answer can be silence.

Choices are placed in front of us every day when we are leaders. Not everything that happens to us is positive, but the good news is that we always have a choice in how we react. There are several paths to travel as a leader.

Let's discuss two paths...

One path is that of the "alligator arms" leader. It is safe and many travel it. It is said that the alligator arms leader operates in *a state in which an individual does not travel nor reach outside of their comfort zone; therefore, they stay within what they view as safe and secure.*

These leaders:

- Protect their money by rarely reaching for the check at lunch meetings.
- Avoid deep conversations.
- Live by their title.
- Avoid risks.
- Do things that are beneficial and safe for them.
- Remain with an organization as long as it is strong.
- Allow others to take blame.
- Redirect to others.
- Spend hours seeking their staff's opinions to assure their own safety.
- Willingly delegate their duties to others. ("Delegation" in this sense is not synonymous with "empowerment.")

Another path, which is less traveled because it involves risks and creates the need for the leader to stretch beyond their comfort zone, is the path of the "orangutan arms" leader, who operates in *a state in which an individual's arms are opened wide to encompass the whole situation.*

If your arms are opened wide, your mind will follow.

These leaders:

- Take time to self-evaluate their part in the failed situation and start again.
- Listen and seek wisdom.
- Reach into their pockets of experience and give all they have.
- Provide appropriate tools needed to maneuver.
- Teach the way to go.
- Encourage with notes, hope, smiles and positive words.
- Let associates shine.

There are many avenues to take. These are only two. The choice is in your hands!

    A local leader called me to share their disappointment in one of their employees. They wanted me to hear the failings of this individual they had put into an important position only 80 days before! When I asked this local leader what approaches and plan of actions they had implemented to help this department leader succeed, they quickly let me know that to do anything would have been a waste of time because it was useless to try to salvage someone who was so obviously inept.

    After around 20 minutes of nonstop talking, this leader thanked me for my help and hung up. I had said nothing! The best help in my mind that I could give this leader was silence.

An individual who is not devoted to the cause has no ears to hear and nothing to develop.

1. Where would you classify this leader who called me?
2. Why do you think they called me?
3. How would you have responded to them?
4. Was silence truly my best response?
5. It is said that silence is good when no one is listening, but how do you know if they are listening?

If the making of a company lies within the hands of the leader:

- What avenue do you want to see leaders travel?
- What leader do you want to follow?
- Which path will you choose to travel as a leader?

CHAPTER 5

Perspective Is Relative

"When you look at a raccoon and see a cat, then it is a cat!"

Not long ago, I spoke with an RN who has worked hard to rise to the position of director of Nursing. She called me because she was hurt and wanted to share a situation in the hopes that I might offer a different perspective.

This nurse worked for a single-owner facility. She was working hard to clear this facility's issues and get the team engaged. During her limited time at the facility, an incident occurred that resulted in an injury to a resident. This nurse immediately instituted a performance improvement program. Her perspective was that the facility needed to communicate that they recognized the error and were working on correcting the situation so it wouldn't happen in the future.

However, the person she reported to had a different perspective. His plans included Wite-Out™! *The administrator was going to take care of the resident and implement a performance improvement program; however, he wanted this nursing director to revise the documentation in the chart so the facility would not be fined.*

I sat listening to her and scratched my head, wondering how any of this could be true. The nurse refused to alter the documentation and she definitely refused to use Wite-Out. Therefore, the owner of the facility immediately fired her and asked her to leave the premises.

Once gone, the nurse started to doubt her decision and began to feel like maybe she did something wrong. She went on to say that perhaps she overreacted. The administrator *was* going to take care of the resident, after all, and no one was really going to be hurt. She continued to say how hard the facility was working to get on the right path, and that it would be difficult to cover the fines and also keep the facility open.

I asked her, "In your mind, does the facility need attention?" She agreed that it did. Then I asked, "Did the state just walk right in and implement fines, or did they give the facility opportunities to correct matters?" She stated they were given opportunities. I asked her then what the organization had done to correct matters to avoid fines. She said the owner said they had been threatened before, but the state usually backed down because there were not enough facilities in the area. The owner told her the state knew the residents needed a place to be and this facility was willing to take them in. With that frame of mind, the facility had done nothing to correct any issues!

It appeared the owner had a myopic view. What I heard was an owner stating his view of the situation: The state needed their facility, so they did not really have to change. In the owner's mind, he took care of these residents, and the state was lucky he provided a place for these types of residents to stay.

I told the nurse that I appreciated her caring attitude, and that I also recognized there were *not* a lot of facilities in her area of the state. Therefore, her leaving this facility would mean she was going to have to travel further to get another position. However, I told her that knowing her the way I did, I thought if she went back to the facility and asked for her job back by stating that she understood why they asked her to do what they did, it would eventually eat her alive.

I acknowledged the administrator was not going to neglect the resident and was going to implement a performance improvement program, but he was still in the wrong. And if he was asking her to falsify records, what else was he doing? My suggestion to her was to follow the guidelines in the Nurse Practice Act, which relates to when a nurse is confronted with an unethical situation.

This nurse could either look at the glass as half full or half empty. Not every firing is a bad thing. Sometimes you are fired because you are in the wrong place and your caring heart is holding you back when God wants you to move on.

The bottom line was this owner didn't recognize that what he was doing was wrong. If he looked at things this way even after the state had warned him several times, then it was highly likely that he was always going to see things the way he was seeing them now.

You have probably figured out by now that this nurse did not go back and she did what was right. She updated her resume and went looking for another position. She presented herself with confidence, she did not lie, she let the other organizations know she was fired, and she made sure she did not speak negatively about the place she left. She let her abilities shine and found out there were organizations that wanted her.

If people are put in a position that doesn't line up with their ethics, they need to say goodbye and move on. Don't beat yourself up; rather, pat yourself on the back and take pride in the fact you got fired. The one who got fired for being asked to do something unethical has just been released to take his or her positive energy to a company where Wite-Out does not exist.

One very positive thing about Electronic Health Records: Wite-Out doesn't work, and the electronic date stamp makes it hard to falsify and back date.

You can tell yourself that what you're doing is OK long enough that you finally start to believe it, but that doesn't alter the fact that "wrong is wrong."

Perspective comes from within a person. Your viewpoint is formed foremost from where you are standing in an organization and life; then it is formed by your personality, moral compass, strengths, fears and emotional intelligence. Perspective is your internal alarm telling you that you are OK, move to the left or right, or "Get the hay out of there." Once that perspective has been clouded, *it is hard – but not impossible* – to get it clear again.

A book worth reading is "Outrageous Love, Transforming Power" by Dr. Terry Wardle, professor of Spiritual Formation at Ashland Theological Seminary in Ashland, Ohio. In his book, Dr. Wardle takes you on a more spiritual journey. He teaches you how to go beyond what we have discussed in this book about personality traits, IQ and EI. He teaches you to identify your spiritual core characteristics and to learn that your core characteristics are nonnegotiable throughout your life. He says, "Never place your identity in anything you can lose." When you are put in an unethical situation like the nurse I spoke of earlier in this chapter, your core characteristics will dictate your immediate reaction.

Studies have revealed that the one thing that sounds the death knell of those who aspire to the top rung of the ladder is *betraying a trust.* It is stated that virtually anything else can be overcome over a period of time, but once trust is betrayed, moving to the top of the ladder is out of the question.

Perspective can also have a fun side. This is a true happening:

It was a bright, sunny autumn day and I was just getting to work. Standing at the nurses' station to greet me was Zena (name changed for privacy), one of our facility's residents. She had a big smile on her face and was dressed for the day. As I approached her, she said, "Hi, Ms. T." As I said "hi" back, I noticed Zena's shoes were on the wrong feet. I told her she looked really nice, and we exchanged some pleasantries about the weather. As I walked away, I told Zena she may want to check her shoes because they appeared to be on the wrong feet.

Zena looked at me with puzzlement in her eyes. Then she looked at her feet, then back at me, then at her feet again, then finally back at me and stated firmly and clearly... "No, those are my feet."

How we view a situation does depend on what role we play in the situation; therefore, it should not be a surprise that everyone on the team is not going to view everything the same way. Zena was looking at her feet because I said her shoes were on the wrong *feet*; however, I was looking at her *shoes*. Two totally different perspectives – yet neither one of us were wrong.

Perceptions do paint pictures, but if you want to be a leader, you need to be more than just perceived as a leader.

Identifying a leader can be as easy as identifying a wart on the tip of a person's nose! The leader is the individual others are following. *Neither a title nor a perception can make a leader,* '*Followers' do!*

If you break it down, there are *only two types* of leaders:
- Constructive (productive)
- Destructive (nonproductive)

There are a multitude of different styles of leadership, but it all boils down to whether you are being constructive or destructive, productive or nonproductive! The question is: *Are you working for the good of the whole, or are you working for the good of yourself? Good or evil?*

Jim Collins (author of "From Good to Great") conducted a study on successful leaders in successful companies over several years. His study revealed two unifying concepts that all "Level 5" (the highest level) leaders had in common.

Those concepts were:
- Passion for the work
- Humility

"Great leaders are almost always great simplifiers, who can cut through argument, debate and doubt to offer a solution everybody can understand." —General Colin Powell

Associates buy into the person before they buy into the leader in the person; therefore, ask yourself:

1. Do you have a vision, and have you been able to share it with others? Are they excited to achieve what you see?
2. Is your passion contagious?
3. Do you genuinely care about those you work with?
4. Do you make leadership decisions that benefit all involved?
5. Do you live what you teach?
6. Are your core characteristics transparent? Honest?
7. Do you make yourself vulnerable?

8. Do you admit mistakes?
9. Do you invest your time into those you work with?
10. When was the last time you went the extra mile?

After you answer the above questions, ask yourself if there is anything you need to change about yourself before you ask your associates to accept you as a leader.

Do you have influence with your associates? Or are they following you because you sign their paychecks?

Leaders without influence are like leaders without followers; they are accomplishing nothing.

To keep staff motivated, leaders need to use their *influence* to convince staff that the organization for which they work is real and is ethical enough for them to buy in.

Here are five tips for attaining influence as the leader:

1. Care about the associates you work with. You have probably heard what I am about to share many times, and you will probably hear it again in the future. But it is **true**. *Staff will not care until they know you care.*

2. Interact with your associates, find out the different reasons they are there and work with them to attain their goals and fulfill their needs.

3. Be honest, and communicate clearly and often. If you don't communicate well, associates will start to communicate among themselves in what they call "the underground network"! Without clear communications, staff will start to fear that their jobs are threatened.

4. Stand up for your associates and acknowledge their successes in front of the team, in front of families and in front of corporate. Create an environment of mutual respect, where individuality, initiative and fresh ideas are welcomed. Take action against team members who are sabotaging the efforts of the whole.

5. Set achievable goals, both short- and long-term. Staying excited requires frequent tastes of victory.

"If your actions inspire others to dream more, do more and become more, you are a leader." —John Quincy Adams

Do you have the intuitiveness to see what motivates associates?

Motives may bring associates in the door but a need that is met keeps them!

- A tack on a chair will get a person to move, but with time, the tack can be removed and the person will go back to sitting.

- Misery, like a tack, can motivate people. However, eventually people will get tired of being miserable and take action. When this happens, the leader needs to direct the associates' energy toward positive actions that will not only improve their current situation but also enable them to live a better life in the future.

- Money motivates people. When money is the motivator, the person looking only at the money will never find true satisfaction. These individuals will stay as long as you pay them well and reward them amply. But as soon as someone else offers them a better package, they will be off to a new setting. These individuals are ones that get to be known as job-hoppers, constantly seeking the pot of gold at the end of the rainbow.

- Individuals who find motivation in being involved in something that will make a significant difference will be the associates who stay. These individuals will stay as long as the leader provides opportunities for them to make lasting differences.

- According to study after study, the motivator that most associates look for is to be recognized publicly for their input and to hear loudly that their work was needed in order for the accomplishment to be achieved. The best rewards for these types of individuals are not monetary.

"Of course motivation is not permanent. But then, neither is bathing; but it is something you should do on a regular basis." —Zig Ziglar

Remember that fear is a perspective and that challenges usually come wrapped in fear. However, after being knocked on your knees a few times, you will start to look at fear in a new light and find it is nothing but a lack of knowledge.

To avoid the onslaught of fear when you take on a new project or become the manager of a new department, you might want to consider building your platform by implementing the following to-do list to assure your associates stay motivated:

1. Look at every process to see what is working and what is not.
2. Ask a lot of questions about things that you don't see set up or that are not self-explanatory.
3. Improve what you can quickly (known as low-hanging fruit), and set goals to work on the things that will take time. Place deadlines on each objective.
4. Communicate and define every player's responsibilities. *Without responsibility, there is no accountability.*
5. Write things down clearly. Write it as many times as it takes to get everyone on the team on the same page. The written word is seldom misunderstood, but sometimes you have to find the *understandable language*. When you want staff to see an apple, you do not want to say "fruit" – they might instead see an orange.
6. Read and study everything you can get your hands on that will improve your knowledge of your new project or department. Self-improvement is a sign of a good leader.
7. Ask yourself, "What do I bring to the table?"
8. Teach the way to success and acknowledge every team accomplishment. No accomplishment is too small to acknowledge.

9. Observe the strengths of each player and build upon those strengths. Mentor, delegate and develop future leaders.
10. Say "thank you" as many times as you possibly can in a day. False platitudes are like ships without rudders; they will set you afloat but with no specific destination.

Implement these points and your team will receive apples when they want apples and not have to deal with an occasional orange!

CHAPTER 6

Cornerstone

"The first stone laid will define the structure."

Over the Christmas holidays, I watched several football games. As I watched the different teams play, it was easy to spot those that had been together a while; the teams that had some seasoned players and some rookies; and, sadly, the teams that had simply been thrown together.

One team I watched had a proven quarterback; however, the receivers and linemen were new. The quarterback was being sacked right and left because the linemen were unable to hold the line. If the quarterback did get a throw off, the receivers had trouble holding onto the ball. On another team, the receivers were in place and open, but the quarterback hesitated too long.

As I watched the various teams play, my thoughts drifted, and I began to think how much work teams are like sports teams. Each player/worker has a position, and that position comes with duties and responsibilities. If just one player/worker is not functioning well or not being responsible, that player/worker can affect the outcome for the entire team.

I watched a team that in the past had been a contender for the Super Bowl several times, but this year their fumbling and frequent missed throws were going to keep them on the sidelines. It appeared as if this team was not communicating. The owner was interviewed, and he was behind his players 100 percent. However, the owner's enthusiasm and support were not enough to carry the team forward to victory.

Another team had lost year after year, but this year they were headed to the playoffs. I found myself cheering for this particular team, even though they were not my home team. I admired their tenacity. The owner did not give up on them, and the team did not give up on themselves. For years, players had come and gone, but finally the mix was right and the team was moving forward.

Companies, like sport teams, have good years and bad years; however, if the players/workers stay together long enough, and they all are able to keep their eyes on the objective, they will taste victory.

In 2013, the Boston Red Sox tasted victory by winning the World Series in baseball. To get to this victory, they had to strip themselves down to nothing and start over again with a new group of players who adopted the concept of team rather than self-importance. The Red Sox front office put their faith in the coach and backed his changes. High-cost players were replaced with lower-cost players! It was a gamble, but the coach stated it had to be a done to paint a new vision. And it worked!

Sometimes drastic actions have to be taken to turn a situation to good. Unfortunately, there are times good employees have to be replaced because they represent the old regime, not because they are bad.

Unfortunately, there are organizations that build their foundation on dishonest practices and no matter what they do to justify their actions they will bear fruit that is rotten.

"You can fool all the people some of the time and you can fool some of the people all of the time. But you cannot fool all of the people all of the time." —Abraham Lincoln

The foolish think the truth will never come out; the wise, however, know that it will, and that lies will beget lies. Build your foundation on truth and honest practices, and you will bear sweet fruit that will become a lasting legacy.

If you are working for an organization that you are not proud to represent, then you need to move on. No matter how hard you work to make your facility strong, the parent company still has control.

I once worked with a young man whose tendencies were to believe the only way to get a client to work with us was through manipulation. When I would speak with him, he excused his behavior by saying he was doing it for the company. However, it was never about the company; it was about him. The day came when I had to wake up, open the door and let him go. The two of us were never going to see things eye to eye. Our perceptions of life were not the same, and no matter what I said, his perceptions of things were the truth to him, and mine were truth to me.

I knew this termination was going to disrupt our entire organization and definitely hurt us financially. We would have to completely reorganize. Knowing all of this, I dragged my feet far too long. I kept telling myself it would all get better. Nothing that is as opposite as black is to white and cold is to hot will get better by ignoring it. Waiting only allows more damage to occur.

I cannot undo my procrastination, but I can learn from it and I certainly can avoid going down that trail again. I am not proud that it took me so long to act. **I had gotten comfortable and let my justifications cloud my vision.**

If you are:

- Offering excuses for unethical behavior
- Stepping in and correcting things to make the company or leader look better
- Telling yourself with time things will come around
- etc.

…it doesn't matter what you tell yourself. Truth is truth. Don't be a fool and don't compromise your beliefs. Take action and change your world.

"For what does it profit a man to gain the whole world and forfeit his soul?" —Mark 8:36

How did I allow myself to get into this situation? Good question – no logical answer. Once I got over the embarrassment of the fact that I let it happen, I picked myself up, paid the consequences, went out and built a better team. I had to roll up my sleeves and put myself back into the quagmire of daily operations. But from the ashes of procrastination came a team with more wisdom.

Financially, my company did take a hit but my family put their faith and support behind me. They helped me keep my eyes on Jesus, and He did not let me drown!

Can good come out of adversity? Yes ... if you handle it with a positive attitude.

I found I could build a team again from scratch. My ways and techniques are solid. They work! Perhaps I should write a book!

The best gift of all is the team that came out of the reconstruction. It is the best team I have ever worked with in my life and we are a better company from the stand I had to take.

Financially, we are well again and I am back to dreaming.

My recommendation to you to avoid having to reorganize your life is when you come across situations like the one I just shared, wake up quickly, separate yourself and move on. Keep your Visine® close by!

If you find you have joined an organization that has not turned out to be all it was presented to be, unless you are going to buy it, you need to sit down have a discussion with your boss and see what can be done to get you both on the same page! If that's not possible, then move on.

In the beginning years, I worked for an organization that asked me to fill in holes on the med and treatment Kardexes with my initials so they would not lose revenue. They told me if I did not do as they asked, then they could not promise that *things would continue to be comfortable for me.* They didn't out-and-out threaten me, because that's against the law, but the handwriting was on the wall. I resigned. Was it fair? No. Was I upset? Absolutely. Had this facility just experienced its first "zero" deficiency survey under my leadership? Yes! Did it matter? Not at all! When I turned in my resignation, this organization told me that I was a poor director of nurses and that I should consider not working in this role in the future. They stated I lacked the ability to see the big picture.

What a hoot. Good thing I knew better than to listen to their evaluation of my abilities. This company is still operating; however, now I have the ability to direct good leaders away from organizations like this one. I guess justice does come if you let go and move on. God will take care of it!

Considering you will spend 75 percent of your time at work, *perhaps* when you are looking for an organization to work for, *you should look at them like you would someone you are starting to date:*

1. Do they conduct themselves in an honest and respectful way in the community? Do others in the community know them and talk positively about them?
2. Is their aroma pleasing? Do they look nice (not that you are basing everything on looks, but do they do the best with what they have?)? Are their surroundings clean and well kept?
3. On your first date, did they listen to you and give you ample time to share? Did they genuinely appear to care about you? Did they tell you about themselves and their accomplishments? Did they share their vision for the future and how they plan to get there? Could you understand those plans, and did you find their vision of their future realistic and attainable?
4. After the first date, did they keep the lines of communication open to you? Were they accessible in more than one way? Did they reflect back to you what they had learned about you and what they appreciated about you? Were opportunities afforded to you to ask more questions about them?
5. Are they a talented and contributing adult in society? Do they have other talented individuals in their family that make you want to go deeper and know them all better?
6. Do they come from a family with a solid and ethical foundation? Can you see and hear their family roots in the community?

Before you get engaged to any person or organization, you want to know if you are appreciated for your individuality. You don't want to jump into a situation where you will suffer heartache later.

Keep your ears open. Talk does circulate, and if the facility and the owners are ethical, the talk will remain positive; conversely, if they are playing a game and are insincere, the truth will come out.

Many voters did not give substance to the rumors circulating about Bill Clinton and his philandering ways with women. His promoters worked hard to cover up his affairs to get him elected. With time, however, Clinton lived up to his reputation. He became comfortable and let his guard down, and my guess is he developed an entitlement attitude, which led him to become the second president in the history of the United States of America to be impeached!

I realize there will be times some of you will join a company because you need a job, and money will be your driving force. But remember that money is only a temporary fix. While you are there, though, you are *still you and your reputation will follow you*; do the best you can with the hand you have been dealt!

Even in times of desperation, look for these six basic properties:

- Foundation built on integrity
- Proven, strong, caring leaders
- Open communications
- Passion for the services provided
- Vision that goes further than the present
- Respect and recognition for individuality

Once you accept a position with a company, and for as long as they sign your paycheck, the talk that comes out of your mouth about the company should be positive. *If you can't say anything positive, then say nothing at all.*

Your reputation is one of your most precious commodities; therefore, keep it positive and dependable.

My husband keeps the following saying framed and on his wall at work. He has lived by these words, and they have served him well!

Loyalty

If – you work for a man, in heaven's name, work for him. Speak well of him and stand by the institution he represents.

Remember – An ounce of loyalty is worth a pound of cleverness.

If - you must growl, condemn and eternally find fault, then resign your position. Once you are on the outside, damn to your heart's content – but as long as you are a part of the institution, do not condemn it. If you do, the first high wind that comes along will blow you away, and probably you will never know why. —Elbert Hubbard

"Only to the extent that men desire peace and brotherhood can the world be made better. No peace, even though temporarily obtained, will be permanent, whether to individuals or nations, unless it is built upon the solid foundation of eternal principles." —*David O. McKay*

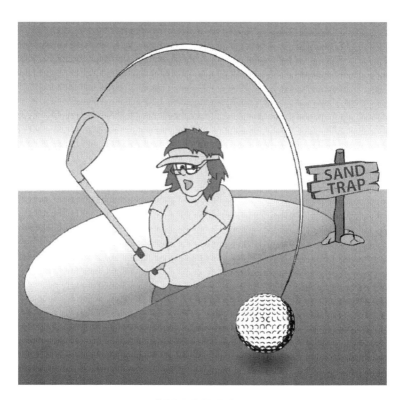

CHAPTER 7

Sand Traps

*"It is not so important why you fall;
it is important that you get up!"*

If you golf, you know what a sand trap is, and you know if you don't focus on your game and the destination of your ball, you can end up in one. Sand traps can be easy to get into but not so easy to get out of. However, with skill and practice, you can learn to avoid sand traps, and if you find yourself in one, the same skill and practice will help you get out.

In the game of leadership, as in the game of golf, leaders can end up in a sand trap faster than they can blink when they take their eyes off the objective. Sand traps come up on you subtly, but before you know it, you are knee-deep in sand.

5 Sand Traps to Avoid in Leadership:

1. Being too "nice," and trying to please everybody.

You want associates to know you care; however, you can go overboard with the niceness! Be real. If associates aren't living up to their expectations, you as the leader have to sit with them and talk. If all you do is encourage your associates to do well but do not hold them responsible, you will get the reputation of being a cheerleader with no substance or a figurehead with no spine.

Challenging associates to accomplish their objectives is a huge part of a leader's responsibilities. Holding them responsible when they are not participating to their fullest is as essential as water is to a tomato plant (if you want tomatoes). If you want your associates to grow, then you have to hold them accountable. Without accountability, you will end up with chaos, mediocrity, complacency, gossip, division, apathy, etc. *And all you were trying to do was be nice.*

Scenario:

You have a new associate call off for the first time. You take the call and tell them you understand, and that is the end of your conversation.

Next day the associate comes in. They do not mention their call-off and neither do you.

The next week, this associate calls off again. Again, you want to appear that you are sympathetic and do not challenge this associate.

Next day, again nothing is said.

This associate calls off for his or her weekend. You tell the associate the two of you need to talk. They become irritated on the phone and state, "You just don't understand," and hang up.

On Monday, you meet with this associate, and they come in with an attitude. You bring up the rules related to call-offs. They start to tell you how bad things are in their life: They don't always have a way to work, sometimes they don't have someone to help with the children, etc. (the dog died, the cat bit the dog, the sun did not come out, they chipped a fingernail – you name it).

They challenge you by saying that you did not mention anything before, so why are you bringing it up now? They accuse you of not understanding and helping them so they can be successful.

How do you handle this situation?

Questions:

- Why did you not say anything at the beginning with the first call-off? Why did you wait until the third call-off?

- What message did this send to the other team members?

- Which of this associate's life issues are your responsibility?

Let's go back now.

Say you did approach the new associate with the rules that govern call-offs from the first call, and when you met with them, they told you all of their problems.

Do you think you the conversation would have gone the same way?

Question:

- Would you have offered to help them with their issues?

It is good to be there for your associates *but if you go through the actions of helping* and they don't take the controls to change what is happening in their life ... where do you think you will end up with this associate?

Protocols are set in place to be followed. If we don't need protocols, then why enact them? You enact them because protocols have been proven. If you let associates know right up front that you expect them at work when they are scheduled, you will communicate a clear message that those in your department take their responsibilities seriously, and you expect new associates to do the same.

To wait and ignore a call-off says to your current hardworking staff that you are not invested in them.

Unless you gave birth to the associate, picked out their spouse or significant other, or make their choices on how they spend their money, you don't own any of the responsibility to solve their problems. Help them, yes, but carry them, no!

If I have heard it once, I have heard it a thousand times: Many leaders are afraid to hold staff accountable to work their shifts because they are afraid the staff will quit and they will be left with no one other than themselves to work the shifts. This is known as entrapment. **When you are encompassed in fear, you are in a downward spiral that won't stop until you make a decision to take a stand.** I know it's difficult, but you must be willing to work those shifts rather than let the undedicated associates have the controls.

I realize as a manager/leader, you cannot work every shift, but stands have to be taken. To solve this issue, you will need the support of your supervisor and all the other supervisors in the facility. You need to meet with them, explain what is going on and discuss an action plan. By joining forces with your supervisor and peers, the message will get out that you are not standing alone. The problem arises when you cannot get your supervisor's support.

At this time, you need to take a serious look at your motives for continuing in your position.

I said this in "Delegate or Suffocate," and I will say it again: Once you take a stand and fire one or two associates for poor attendance or poor attitude, the others will begin to respect you because they know you really do care and you do mean business.

There is no reason you have to be rude or mean when you fire an individual. Just keep in mind that you are not really firing these associates. They are firing themselves! They were the ones who did not want to work at the facility or on the unit. They were the ones causing issues. They may not be literally shouting that they do not like this place and they want a change, but their actions are shouting it loudly. Open the door and let them have their change!

A big sand trap when you are reaching out to associates who have a lot of issues at home is to offer to help them get out of their issues. Remember that only they can take control of their issues. They created them and they will have to resolve them. If they don't take responsibility and ownership of their problems, they will remain crippled for life. *Learning how to climb above problems strengthens your legs, and then those legs can take you farther than you ever thought possible.*

Your response should be more on the level of, "Now that we have discussed what's going on, what do you believe *you* can do to change your predicament?" As a leader, you want to care about your associates and their individual situations. You do want to talk and see the situation from their perspective. The fine line you don't want to cross is becoming an *enabler!* Make some suggestions based on your understanding of what's happening, but don't volunteer to ease their burden by taking on their responsibilities. Keep the focus on them and their ability to solve things through their own initiative. Keep the conversation positive and assure them you have the confidence that the issues can be worked out.

You may have to adjust their schedule to meet what they know they can fulfill. This doesn't mean they never have to work weekends, but if an employee can work every Tuesday and Friday but is having trouble with Mondays and Thursdays, perhaps there is another individual who can handle Monday and Thursday. I am not saying for you to adjust the schedule to meet the needs of one, but I am suggesting you open it up so that the associates can exchange their schedules. For added security in this situation, have both associates sign off on any exchanged commitments.

"I cannot give you the formula for success, but I can give you the formula for failure, which is: Try to please everybody." —Herbert Swope

As the leader, you will want to align your associates into four basic categories:

    A. Unofficial leaders

    B. "Woe is me" victims

    C. Superheroes (the rescuers)

    D. Engaged associates

A. Unofficial Leaders
Characteristics:

- Expressive and sarcastic
- Poor listener
- Pushes others' buttons

The unofficial leader can often be seen as a bully to their coworkers. The interesting thing about these leaders is that they can be productive; unfortunately, though, it is usually production at the cost of others' morale. These unofficial leaders often become the associate promoted into management by leaders who want to keep production up but are not looking at operations as a whole. Once these individuals are official leaders, the organization usually starts to experience increased turnover.

Suggestions to make this negative a positive:
- ✓ Give these individuals your undivided attention in your office.
- ✓ Let them express themselves without interrupting them or trying to correct their view.
- ✓ Once they have expressed themselves thoroughly, summarize what you've heard and come up with an agreed list of issues.
- ✓ Now prioritize together, and come up with the most important issue that needs to be worked on.
- ✓ Do not change protocols unless it makes sense to do so.
- ✓ The key is not to embarrass this individual but to help them learn to contribute in a positive tone.
- ✓ Take the time to mentor and develop this person into an effective leader. This happens when you let them contribute and receive recognition for their contribution.

B. "Woe Is Me" Victims

Characteristics:
- Quiet
- Embellish issues and situations
- Blame others for their problems

Victims always have an excuse as to why they can't complete their assignments or have to call off. Their fingers automatically point away from themselves. To accept responsibility for their life and the happenings that are occurring in their life would mean they could possibly change their conditions. Positive goals are an extremely foreign thought for them.

Suggestions to make this negative a positive:

- ✓ As with the unofficial leader, these individuals need to have one-on-one time with you. They need to express themselves.
- ✓ Don't interrupt them but do provide feedback of what you hear them saying. Wait for validation.
- ✓ Make sure you relate to them in an empathetic way, but do not take their issues on as your – or the organization's – issues.
- ✓ Prioritize their issues with their help, and ask them to identify which one needs to be worked on first.
- ✓ Then discuss how they are going to make things better. It's OK to mention organizations that can help them, but it needs to be them who make the calls to get help.
- ✓ Set the expectation that each time you meet with them over an issue, they will come with at least one solution.
- ✓ Recognize their achievements, and give them opportunities to score quick wins to build their view of their possibilities.

C. Superheroes – Rescuers

Characteristics:

- Overextended
- Focused more on others' assignments than their own
- Love to be loved… they judge themselves by what others say about them

At first, rescuers are loved by everyone; eventually, however, coworkers find this person "talks the talk" but doesn't "walk the talk." They overcommit to all and end up not delivering! That doesn't, however, stop them from trying to save everyone. They tend to bend the rules to make others feel OK about not doing their jobs completely. They have an overinflated opinion of themselves and what they think is right and wrong.

Suggestions to make this negative a positive:

- ✓ Like all associates, superheroes need one-on-one time with their leader. They need to express themselves.
- ✓ Listen well and reflect your appreciation for their efforts to help everyone.
- ✓ However, you need to help them break down their responsibilities and teach them how important it is for them to accomplish their duties so that everyone can shine. Publicly acknowledge their contributions.
- ✓ Teach and mentor them that by doing too much for others, they cripple them and take away that individual's opportunity to grow and advance in their position.
- ✓ Rescuers make good trainers. Assign them to be mentors. This will tend to focus their energy into a smaller area – namely, one associate.

D. Engaged Associates

Characteristics:

- Confident
- Productive
- Encouraging

Engaged associates are those who look for ways for everyone to shine. They recognize their part on the team and know they are important. They are self-motivated, and they contribute to the success of projects.

What do you do with an engaged associate?
- ✓ Feed them.
- ✓ Mentor them.
- ✓ Open doors for them.
- ✓ Give them public recognition.
- ✓ Challenge them.
- ✓ Empower them.
- ✓ Give them one-on-one time with you.
- ✓ Find a way to multiple them.

What these different associates in the four categories are doing is natural to them; therefore, they think they are doing well. They need you as their leader to give them the expert guidance they need to develop and turn negative behaviors into positive actions. *It will take time and energy, but it is possible!*

2. Not letting go and delegating.

A constructive leader will let go and delegate because they know this action will increase productivity and develop more leaders. Constructive leaders not only delegate; they also empower.

Leadership Style	**Constructive**
Motivation	Positive, inspires, empowers
Vision	Long-term focus with short-term successes
Results	Mentoring, high productivity, loyal staff
Environment	Trust and openness
Effects	Promotes win-win

There can be three motives to not delegating:
1. You do not trust others to complete the task.
2. You like having all the control and having everyone come to you.
3. You are afraid if everyone can function without you, there will be no need for you.

We had an individual on our team who said she wanted others to be successful; she taught new associates what to do and then she would send them off to do what she had taught them. When the associates would return with a candidate they thought could fill an open position, the leader, instead of moving forward to the next step with the candidate, would question the associate on every point they were to cover with the candidate. On top of the questions, this leader would double-check the associate to make sure everything was indeed asked and the answers were substantial.

The leader thought she was "letting go" because she did not call the candidate back directly and re-ask the questions. She did accept the candidates the associates brought her, but only after her questions were answered to her satisfaction. This leader "let go" of the task of actually making calls, but did not relay trust to her associates by just accepting what they had to say. The associates got the impression the leader didn't think they knew what they were doing.

This is one of those incidents where it may appear as if you are letting go, but you are not! The multiple questions and double-checking are loudly stating to your staff, "I don't trust your judgment, and I feel the need to double-check you."

When you delegate, you have to let go and be OK if they fall, and be willing to go down with them. If you have taught them well, they will not fall. That is why you teach and then let go – not the other way around. Let go and let them learn to bounce back if and when they fall.

This leader needed a little tweaking. I met with her and gave her a roll of duct tape. She looked at me puzzled, but I told her I wanted her to keep it on her desk to remind her to cover her mouth and trust what the associates brought her and believe that she did a great job teaching them. This leader laughed but she got the point. Her production increased because she put more workers in the field to harvest the candidates.

This leader's personality trait causes her to battle with letting go. She is an achiever. And as we discussed earlier in this book, personality traits are hard to change. She came from an environment that was very competitive, where everyone worked in isolation. With time, training and a new environment, this leader has learned that she may not be able to change her personality trait but she can improve her Emotional Intelligence. Her improved EI has shown her the huge benefit in giving others the opportunity to shine.

Delegation is the beginning of letting go, but the final step is empowerment. Knowing the difference is helpful:

<u>Delegation</u>	<u>Empowerment</u>
Here's what I need from you	What do you need from me?
This is how you do it	This is your role
This is what I want it to look like	This is where we're going
This is what you need to do next	Your work fits into the big picture
I'll give you the last 5%	I'll let you contribute the last 5%
I own it	You own it
Here's where I see this going	Where do you see this going?
Concrete	Fluid
Toe the company line	Pushback is encouraged
Tasks	Results
No room for other leaders	Room for other leaders
Guided by preference	Guided by values
Here's my opinion	What's your opinion?

3. Overdoing meetings and paperwork.

When I was a regional nurse, I worked with a regional director of operations (RDO) who showed up to every meeting the region held with a ton of paperwork. I looked at him in amazement and wondered how many trees he must be killing each day by printing all those paper reports. I had to admit, though, he knew absolutely everything that was going on in his region.

Unfortunately, his knowledge came at a cost. He was on high-blood pressure and anti-anxiety medications. He thought if he knew everything, his region would shine; therefore, he spent his day consumed with reports and conversations with his staff.

This leader failed to see that running the facilities was the job of the administrative staff in the building. His job was to be there to help them with issues that stumped them. A successful leader trusts those they have hired to do their job. They will let go and do their job. The RDO's job was to look for ways to make the administrative team's job easier, not give them unnecessary paperwork. If anything, the goal was to minimize paperwork.

When my associates became proficient at their duties, I found myself looking for things to do, and started looking around to see how I could improve their workplace. What could I request to purchase that would increase the time they had to be more available for the residents/patients and family members?

It eventually came to light that this RDO had a prior bad experience with a micromanager as a boss, and he was trying to make sure he could answer any question that might be asked of him. He didn't want to suffer another humiliation like he had while working with that micromanager. It is amazing the damage that can be done at the hands of a destructive leader.

As a leader, you do want to have meetings because you want to keep the communication lines open. The main objective, however, is not to *overdo* meetings and, for heaven's sake, don't make them long. I was taught in my first psychology class in college that the average adult quits listening after 20 minutes; therefore, it is wiser to have small, frequent meetings than to have one two-hour meeting. If you hold a two-hour meeting, then you have just succeeded in wasting your breath for one-and-a-half hours.

If you start to get a lot of paper reports that you have not requested from an associate, you may want to take some time to have a meeting with this associate. Perhaps he or she worked with a micromanager in the past and needs some reassurance you are OK with their decisions and work habits.

Some associates may send every memo, letter or policy to the leader for approval. You may think that's an acceptable action, but if you didn't ask them to pass everything through you, then you need to meet with them individually and find out why they are behaving in such a manner. You want them to know that when you delegate to them, you trust they can handle the task at hand. It does a leader no good to delegate a task just to have the associate push all the approval back to the leader. An individual conversation will reveal the root cause. Hopefully, you will not find out that they are covering their rear in case things go wrong. Both reasons need to be discussed and settled. If the behavior continues, you may have to consider the possibility that you have delegated a task to them that is above their ability.

4. Being inaccessible; demonstrating poor follow-through.

Your office can become a "safe haven," a place away from all the questions; however, staying in your office also keeps you away from staff interactions.

Every leader needs downtime behind closed doors to concentrate and plan. But if a leader becomes inaccessible, then the momentum will begin to fade, and staff will go back to doing what they were doing before. Ultimately, things will revert to the way they were before any change ever started.

Running into your office and hiding behind a pile of paperwork *closes* the door to the fantastic opportunities to "catch someone doing something right" on your daily walking rounds! Walking rounds are your times to bond with the other associates and build your influence as a leader. When associates see you out and about, they view you as an in-touch leader.

Use your calendar and schedule time each day to go out into the facility and interact with associates, customers, residents/patients and family members. Allot enough time so you can stop and engage in conversations and compliment the good you see.

Closed doors create silos!

When associates ask for clarification and you tell them you will get back to them, *then please get back to them.* If you say you will take care of an issue, *then please take care of the issue.* Once an issue is resolved, inform your teammates you have accomplished what you said you would do, and present them with the results of your actions (negative or positive).

Accountability and communication flow both ways!

When you promise to follow through on something, your associates are counting on you – putting their trust in you. If you don't follow through on a promise or commitment, you lose their trust. That's a commodity no one wants to lose! Please remember when you *betray a trust* as a leader, that is the one action that sounds the death knell for those who aspire to the top rung of the ladder.

I have a friend whom I love dearly, but if you want her to arrive on time, you have to tell her to be there an hour earlier than the actual time. Even though you take this action, there is no guarantee she will arrive on time. She is my friend because she has many other traits that outshine her trait for lateness. However, her lateness and lack of follow-through would prevent me from hiring her to be one of our company's leaders. I know my friend's heart is good, but even when you ask her to do something and she swears she can and will do it, she rarely is able to completely follow through. You forgive someone you care about, but if you have to depend upon that person daily to carry the load, and each day you find you are cleaning up after them, the "care about" instinct begins to grow thin. Even after being friends for years, when my friend fails to follow through, it still makes me wonder how important I am to her. Imagine if I had to report to a leader like her at work.

If you want staff to be on time and to follow through, then you as the leader need to be a role model and set the pace.

Are you setting the pace ...or taking up space?

5. Getting comfortable ...and full of self!

Would you celebrate a survey that states you are in 98 percent compliance? Sound fantastic? Now what if I were to ask you, *"Would you agree to use a parachute from a parachute company that boasts a 98 percent quality guarantee?"*

Oh, so now that 98 percent doesn't sound so fantastic, and you're not rushing to the front of the line!

Many years ago, I heard a story at a conference that I am going to share with you. It had a huge impact on me (but please understand that this was not authored by me!):

The owner of a parachute company was given a quality insurance report, and his staff members were celebrating the fact that their company had achieved 98 percent perfection. Unlike his staff, the owner was not satisfied with the 98 percent. To improve, he decided to implement a new testing program. He required all of his employees to personally test the parachutes before they went on the market for sale. In a very short period of time, the quality improved to 100 percent.

The chicken makes a contribution; the pig makes an investment.

Successful leaders know when they start to think that things will always remain the same, they are headed down a disastrous road. Successful leaders are never content with status quo. They are always looking for ways to improve things for the whole. They thrive on challenges and meeting those challenges.

"You are never too old to set another goal or to dream a new dream." —C. S. Lewis

Have you ever stood in the ocean with the waves flowing in? Are you able to stand in the same spot? If you dig your feet in, what happens? In a constant where the constant is forever changing, there is no way to stand in the same spot without falling over! The deeper you try to dig in, the more your foundation fades!

Life has taught us that our society does not remain the same. If you don't think this is a true statement, then take a look at the most fundamental attire, such as underwear, and tell me if it is the same as it was in 1800. Society changes daily, and those changes cause a domino reaction to many facets of our industry. If leaders fail to look at what is going on in society and are not thinking how their organization can keep up and continue to deliver a quality product, then they are not the leaders you want to follow.

I watched an individual develop in his position. When I first met him, he was a healthcare administrator. He soon achieved the position of regional director of Operations. He eventually was hired to be the chief operations officer of an organization. In a short period of time, he was promoted to chief executive officer. He hired me to help him settle his nursing department. When I first went to his headquarters, he showed me around and introduced me proudly to all the members of his team.

On my next visit, he was calling meetings at different facilities. Upon his arrival, staff would greet him and tell him they had set up the conference room as he had required, and they had the items he wanted to munch on ready on the table. It appeared as if everyone was catering to him and focusing less on the issues.

As I watched him in these meetings, I became sad because he was unaware of what he was doing. He had worked hard to get where he was but now he was falling into one of the ***biggest sand traps of all: pride!*** He had lost sight of where he had come from and how he had gotten into his powerful position. I tried talking to him, but he was as blind as a bat to his behavior!

Eight months later, I saw him at a healthcare convention; he nodded but didn't stop to chat. He was walking alone and his staff was keeping their distance. Assigned staff ate with him, but according to them, he controlled the conversation. As I watched him, the only thought I had was, "Pride cometh before a fall." One month later, he lost his position as CEO.

The demise of a leader is hard to watch, but there is no alternative when a leader starts to think they are the only reason things are well and they need no one. There is no other path left for them to take but the path of ruin!

I lost touch with this individual, but the buzz is he got out of healthcare.

An ounce of prevention is worth a pound of cure:

- Be true to yourself and your beliefs.
- Act in a consistent manner that aligns with your beliefs.
- Speak well of the company you work for. If you are unhappy, discuss it with your superior. If you can't achieve a positive working relationship, then leave.
- Listen to the true intentions of your associates.
- Show you care and appreciate your associates' contributions and individuality.
- Get out and roll up your sleeves once in a while, and do it cheerfully, creating an atmosphere of mutual respect.
- Pay five truthful and non-generic compliments every day.
- Give credit where credit is deserved.
- Mentor, trust your associates, let go and help them grow.
- Keep learning and keep growing. Be a positive, professional role model.
- Never, never think you are the "cat's meow"!
- Know how to say **"Thank you."**

CHAPTER 8

Which Hat Shall I Wear Today?

"You train a dog, but you develop a person!"

Some issues, such as attendance, may appear on the surface to have a black-and-white response. But the path to resolve the issue may not be as clear-cut as it seems.

You have to take into consideration:

- Personality Traits
- Emotional Intelligence
- Strengths
- Innate Qualities
- Core Characteristics
- Experiences
- Tasks To Be Completed
- Level of Understanding
- etc.

Richard and I have two sons. They were born six years apart. I thought since things went so well with William, my years of experience with William would make it easier to raise Christopher. *Wrong!* The boys are alike yet very different. Morally and ethically they are very much the same, but personality-wise, they are night and day.

I could put William in a playpen with a few toys and he was as happy as a tick on a dog. Christopher, however, did not like the confines of a playpen. When I put him in the playpen with a toy, he would throw it out and whine until I pulled him out. William was happy to play alone with his toy soldiers for hours in his room or the family room, whereas Christopher wanted to be where the action was and with others. Christopher loved interaction. Just knowing this little bit, if you were to meet the boys, you would immediately be able to tell which one is which.

When it came to corrective action with the boys, I had to take two totally different approaches to attain the result of compliance. For William, being sent to his room was a treat, while having to sit and watch TV with the family was a burden. For Christopher, being sent to his room was torture. Also, I could be direct with William, and he seldom argued back. Christopher, on the other hand, wanted to rationalize and discuss the practicality of all the house rules.

I share all of this to demonstrate that, even though my quest was to get each of the boys to be home on time, I had to approach them very differently to get those results. It's the same with staff members. You want them to come to work and do their jobs, but your approach in getting them to do so needs to change according to the each associate's personality.

The Personality Plus test will reveal a mix of personality traits in a person. One trait will be more dominant and shine through most often, but rare is the case that two individuals possess the exact same combination of traits. Armed with this knowledge, you can see why there can be no concrete formula to follow when dealing with associates.

In any company, there may be a Sanguine who has an equal strength of Choleric with a small amount of Melancholy and zero Phlegmatic, while another Sanguine has a very high Sanguine and a very low Choleric with zero in the rest. Both individuals will be outgoing, but one of them is not going to have much logic or the take-charge strengths.

Traits plus qualities such as integrity, empathy, honesty, assertiveness, high EI skills, charisma, intuitiveness, etc. are helpful for a leader to have; however, no one trait or combination of qualities guarantees success as a leader.

Once again, leadership styles include the following:

- Transactional
- Autocratic
- Bureaucratic
- Charismatic
- Democratic/Participative

- Laissez-faire
- Task-oriented
- People/Relations-oriented
- Transformational

The **transactional leadership** style works in an organized environment where processes are well spelled out. Associates know what is expected of them if they produce and what will happen to them if they do not produce. This type of leadership tends to reward with bonuses and motivate associates with fear.

The short-term focus of this management style is great for projects. It is effective for individuals who are there to do a job and receive a paycheck. The associates who work well under this type of leadership style don't get caught up in the politics of the organization. They are content to give of their time for pay and then go home and enjoy their lives.

This approach works well getting new employees started, but if continued, it will stunt the growth of associates who could be mentored.

Autocratic leadership, also known as dogmatic leadership, features one – and only one – boss. What this leader says goes, and attempts from associates to negotiate or offer input are not welcome. The positive of this leadership style is that associates definitely understand where they fall on the organizational chart and where they are going to stay at that moment.

Decisions are made quickly, because there is no input from others. This style can be very efficient, but if continued, it leads to high turnover and absenteeism. You see this leadership style in assembly lines, the military and unskilled positions.

This type of approach works well in times of crisis. If a code is called, a leader would use this type of leadership so the associates performing the tasks can keep their focus on the patient/resident. This is also true of troops going into battle. Often you will see this in the kitchen of a restaurant during peak serving time.

The **bureaucratic leadership** style is appreciated by those who are analytical and work in the areas of organizations that rely heavily on proper safety procedures. The associates can predict what will happen to the best of anyone's ability. The rules, however, are usually stern with very little flexibility.

This may be seen by some as paternal leadership: "These rules and protocols are set up to keep you safe, son."

If you work in surgery, you deal with this type of leadership often to assure the area around and near the patient is set up safe and secure for surgery. There is no room for error in surgery. You have rigid rules to adhere to, and there can be no questions as to why they exist. This type of leadership is good when dealing with nuclear energy, the Center for Disease Controls or any environment that has a high degree of risk.

Leaders can use this approach in specific situations, but if they use it under all circumstances, it will lead to turnover and resentment from their associates. In this type of leadership, leaders must demonstrate that they have the same skill required from the associates, or else face possible opposition and/or insubordination.

Charismatic leadership is what it says: The leader is charming. Staff members get drawn into the leader's charisma. Many preachers and movie stars are charismatic. They know how to inspire and motivate.

The area you have to be concerned with in this style of leadership is learning whether the leaders are leading their staff for the good of the whole or for the good of themselves. Staff can become so mesmerized by a charismatic leader that they lose their internal compass. The preacher Jim Jones was a charismatic leader and we all know what happened to those who followed him (in case you do not remember – he convinced his followers to kill themselves).

When an organization needs to make major changes, this type of leadership style is necessary for getting associates excited, engaged and on board.

To keep this type of leadership on board, charismatic leaders need to demonstrate to the staff that their intentions are to help them grow and become all they can be.

The **democratic/participative leadership** style works well if you have time to include everyone in the decision-making process. This is one of the top leadership styles proven to increase staff morale and make associates excited that they belong to the organization.

This leadership style invites input from the associates, welcomes fresh ideas and appreciates creative approaches.

This is a great style to approach in most situations that do not require immediate decisions! When associates know that their input is valued, they have a higher degree of investment. They feel acknowledged and appreciated for their uniqueness.

If there is a downside to this leadership style, it's that the organization has to allot the time it takes for it to work. The organization needs to trust and invest in the leaders and their style to enjoy the fruits of the labor.

With this leadership style, the organization will experience less turnover, improved quality of delivery and higher productivity.

This approach works well with most associates, but if an associate is a task-oriented individual or someone who might not have expertise or a high degree of knowledge of what is going on, you will need to adjust your expectation of their quality of input. You must adjust your expectation and allot all the opportunity to shine.

Laissez-faire leadership is also known as "whatever" leadership. This is where leaders hope all associates know what to do, or, if they don't, where they can go to get the information or knowledge they need.

The work environment under this type of leader is usually chaotic. However, if you work in a department with experienced team members who are highly skilled in their positions, this is a great leadership approach. With team members like that, you want to stay out of their way and let them fly. If they need to talk, this kind of leader will make time for them, but if expert advice is needed, this leader will refer them to another.

The **task-oriented leadership** style is much like the autocratic leadership style. As with autocratic, this style lets you know that even the associates who just like doing tasks and not getting caught up in the creative side of the business can be leaders.

When you put this type of leadership into place, you can bet the tasks will be completed. However, this approach will not work well with someone who wants to fly on his or her own!

People-oriented/Relations-oriented leadership is another style that states exactly what leaders do: They focus on the people in the organization.

They seek the uniqueness and individuality of each person on the team and in the organization, and do what they can to reflect these qualities and traits back to the staff. They are outgoing, approachable and accessible.

This leadership style is like the democratic style. Staff members respond very well to this style of leadership and fight to belong to their teams.

This approach is a good one to use when you are encouraging associates to develop their own ability to resolve an issue. The democratic leaders participate and set an example for other associates to follow. They are the ones who roll up their sleeves once in a while and pitch in for the benefit of everyone. They are not above any position, and you see this in their actions and attitude.

If there is a downside to this leadership style, it would have to be that this type of leader tends to put the needs of the people above the project that needs to be completed. This is why people-oriented/relationship-oriented leaders need to make sure they balance their team members with a task-oriented leader.

Transformational leadership is the type of leadership an organization wants to invest in, because transformational leaders grow other leaders. They grow not only more leaders like themselves but also leaders who represent other leadership styles.

This type of leader has the ability to observe associates, recognize their strengths and inspire them to develop and step up to the plate.

This approach would not work well if the organization is in a crisis situation or involved in reorganization. Most transformational leaders are capable of focusing on what needs to be accomplished and then coming back around and building staff. However, this type of leader will be laying groundwork with everyone on the team from the beginning.

Transformational leaders are visionaries! They look at where the company needs to go and whom they need to hire to reach the objectives.

When it comes to handling management situations, there are no truly simple solutions.

As a leader, you have many facets to take into consideration:

- What training has been provided
- Whether a mentor has been assigned
- What structure was already in place
- What structures need to be changed
- What strengths in this individual made them appear a good candidate for manager
- Whether job descriptions exist
- Whether there are individual job expectations for each position
- What commitment the company has made to support this individual and the actions they may need to take
- etc.

We have discussed the different leadership styles; now, let's discuss a few employee personality styles:

A task-oriented individual... This type of employee functions well under an individual with the personality of Melancholy and an autocratic leadership style. Task-oriented individuals want things clearly spelled out: what time to do the task, what to expect from the task, how many tasks should be completed in a certain allotted time, etc.

Task-oriented individuals don't think well "outside of the box." They like a written protocol for everything. To put an individual such as this in a position that requires making assumptions all day long would not be advantageous for either the individual or the company. Find a routine job that requires the same action most of the day, and you will have a productive, happy camper. These individuals don't like getting caught up in the philosophy of the world; they just want to get the job done.

An achiever/competitor... This individual will want a rulebook and one that is fairly written. An achiever/competitor will want to be given expectations and goal set dates, but after that, will want to be left alone. This individual has personal drive; therefore, you can let go and rest assured expectations will be met before or right on the goal set dates. At this point, this individual would work well even under a laissez-faire leadership style.

This type of individual will set goals to achieve every day and will not leave work until those daily goals have been met.

Achievers/competitors thrive on challenges, so this personality type would appreciate a delegator type of leadership style. A Choleric personality works well with achievers. However, achievers do tend to ask a lot of questions when they are first being presented a challenge, and that behavior can tend to irritate a Choleric. Knowing this bit of information definitely assists in the approach.

Mr. or Ms. Sunshine... These are the individuals who enter a room with a happy saying, and everyone knows they see the glass half-full – *no, wait, they want you to know they see the glass as full as it can possibly be at that moment in time.*

These individuals are "on" all the time. They have endless energy, but they can get lost in a paper bag. They have difficulty pouring water out of a boot with the instructions on the bottom of the heel.

They are communicators and connectors. They look for everyone to be treated fairly and equally. To them, the whole world is in harmony. But good luck if you want this type of individual to focus for a long period of time. Focus is no easy task. Within a few moments of a seminar, these individuals will have their cell phones on and be checking their texts, Facebook, Twitter and emails.

These individuals function best with a participant/ diplomatic style of leadership. Since they are charismatic, putting them with a charismatic leader may cause a clash in who gets the attention. They look for their leaders to sit and go over different approaches with them, and toss out ideas that are fun and unique. They want their leader to dream with them. They are social and like to talk, so they appreciate a leader who knows how to listen and let them express themselves freely.

Analytical...intellectual...strategic... These individuals want to analyze everything and then put the information into policies, procedures, guidelines, objectives, etc. They want every needed action and step backed up with logic and purpose.

These are the individuals who will read every word in a warranty for a set of tires. They will have every possible thing that could go wrong supported with a policy that directs the team on what to do to get out of that situation.

These individuals tend to be skeptics. When you ask them if the cup is half-empty or half-full, they want to know the purpose of your question.

They function best under the guidance of a transactional or bureaucratic leader. They like to work under the leadership of someone who wants to get to the point, identify the issues and fix them. They don't look as much to the future (outside of financial) as they do to the present: They want to know what can be done now that will work.

Quiet as a mouse/thinker... Don't underestimate these individuals! They sit back, but they aren't meek or easily swayed. Like the Phlegmatic, they like peace, order and harmony; however, when the chips are down, they will step up and take charge. They are resolved in their thinking, they have looked at the situation from every angle, and they know who is a true player and who is not. They also know if an issue is solvable or should be thrown out the door.

These individuals are loyal and not limelight seekers. They have your back and will work hard to secure a resolution. They like their family life and don't like having to put in extra hours at work, but they will do it for a short period if they believe the end is worth the sacrifice.

These are great individuals to run your volunteer programs. They will be there, and they will put their team out in front to get the recognition they deserve. They function best with a people/relations-oriented leader. They like to follow someone who is moral and kind to others.

"Woe is me" victim... These individuals can make reasonably good task-worker bees. Their ability to look at the big picture is limited, however. Their focus is on themselves and their comfort. They will not miss a break. If they come in late from an appointment, they will still take their lunch break, even if it's 15 minutes after they arrive.

They struggle to achieve and never see it as their fault when they don't advance. Life is rough for them, and they talk a lot about their sorrows. This is why they work best at tasks that don't require a lot of thought. They are satisfied when they can talk about their problems and still perform their tasks and receive a paycheck.

The best way to approach this person is through a task-oriented leadership style, but you need to be careful not to tread heavily on their feelings. Mixing your approach with some charismatic charm is good for these individuals.

Mover...shaker...visionary...futuristic... These employees come in and take charge. They are good communicators and know how to rally the troops. They exude confidence from every pore in their bodies. You meet them and you want them to lead your team. They are outgoing and display understanding and empathy of the situation.

They usually tell stories to get their points across, and are realistically charismatic. They are not intimidated in social settings, and they like meeting strangers. You put these individuals in a line at a grocery store; they will have no hesitation in starting a conversation. They like hearing other people's points of view. They are not argumentative; in fact, individuals like this can be in a conversation with two people who have completely opposing viewpoints, and each individual will walk away from the conversation thinking that this individual agreed with them.

These employees function best under the transformational leadership style. Tell them what needs to be done, and get out of their way. Put your trust in them and you won't be disappointed. They will work hard, and during the whole process, they will put their focus on building the team and give the team all the glory.

Individuals like these flourish under almost any type of leadership because they are confident in their abilities. However, they will not stay under a leadership style that does not mentor them and enable their development.

There are a multitude of personality styles that I have not covered, but I trust what I have shared will show you what I mean when I say, "One leadership approach will not work for all of the associates on your team."

To be an accomplished leader, you need to take the time to get to know each member of your team. Learn their strengths, personalities, hot buttons, motives, driving forces, interests, living conditions, families, responsibilities outside of home, etc. This will help you identify the appropriate leadership style to use when dealing with the different associates. This will lead to success for all!

For the first time in history, we have four generations (some say there are five, but that is because they break up

Generation X into Y and Z) in the work force at the same time. This alone is a challenge that none before us has had to balance. What worked a generation ago in the work field is no longer effective. More than ever before, leaders have to consider whom they are approaching to achieve desired outcomes. They not only have to take into consideration their associates' personality traits and strengths, but they also have to balance this with their generational influence. I couldn't approach Christopher the same way I approached William because of not only their personality traits but also their age difference. William was born into the Baby Boomer generation while Christopher fell into Generation X.

William grew up when mothers stayed home and all children were seen as special. Christopher grew up with daycare and dual-income families. One of the most popular TV programs when William was young was "Lassie"; with Christopher, it was "Three's Company." I now have grandchildren in the Millennial generation and, God bless them, they are coddled children. My grandchildren think they should get a trophy for just showing up to a game. The popular TV programs for my grandchildren have been "Friends," "The Simpsons" and "South Park." Morals definitely changed from generation to generation. Divorce is not a rare occurrence in the Millennial generation, and what they value is totally different from what Baby Boomers value.

Here are some of the <u>traits</u> you can expect to see from each generation in the work environment:

Traditionalists

- Dedicated
- Believe in having to pay your dues
- Company first
- Respect authority
- Do not take a lot of time off… they work hard to maintain a job and an income for their family

Baby Boomers

- Driven
- Workaholic – 60-hour workweeks are not unusual
- Work long hours to establish self-worth, identity and fulfillment
- Time spent at job equals authority to them… if you haven't been there a long time or done the job, they don't respect what you say
- Don't take a lot of time off for fear they will lose favor with authority or their jobs

Generation X

- Balanced
- Work smarter not harder
- Self-reliant
- Want structure but with some flexibility
- Suspicious and skeptical of authority
- Test authority repeatedly
- Focus on a clearer balance between work and play
- Confident, with no worries about losing their jobs

Millennials

- Ambitious
- Multitaskers
- Tenacious
- Entrepreneurial

- Test authority but do seek out guidance from authority figures
- Want flextime, job sharing, sabbaticals and job development offers

What do they <u>look for in a job</u>?

Traditionalists
- ✓ Recognition and respect for their years of experience
- ✓ Tradition
- ✓ Security and stable environment
- ✓ Rules and protocols
- ✓ Do what is needed to be done … not important whose job it is … it's about the company and achieving good results

Baby Boomers
- ✓ The ability to shine and get a title
- ✓ Opportunities to contribute
- ✓ A company with good values and strong belief in their cause
- ✓ Team approach
- ✓ Job descriptions and expectations
- ✓ Respect for their abilities

Generation X
- ✓ Exciting and dynamic leaders
- ✓ Innovation
- ✓ Cutting-edge systems
- ✓ Forward-thinking organization

- ✓ A culture that judges employees by their input rather than seniority
- ✓ Freedom to express themselves and to question purposes and actions
- ✓ Flexibility in scheduling

Millennials

- ✓ Challenges! (They don't like boring jobs)
- ✓ A positive environment with positive leaders
- ✓ Strong and ethical leaders and mentors
- ✓ Development opportunities that keep them on the cutting edge of what's happening in their industry
- ✓ No hierarchy
- ✓ Flexible schedules
- ✓ Generous pay and options

The differences are not insurmountable, but they place a lot of demands on the leaders of today. The days of the "This is how it is or hit the bricks" approach is gone. Understand and care about your associates, and you will be fine.

CHAPTER 9

Change Starts with YOU!

"I look to my brother and he does not move; shall I sit? But the fire is hot!"

Since I have worked in healthcare most of my adult life, I am going to take the time in this chapter to challenge other leaders in my field. *However, if you are a leader in another field and you are reading my book, I ask that you stop and take a look at what you can do in your industry to improve conditions.* A leader is a leader. The industry is insignificant. Ask yourself what you can do to attract top executives and keep current associates engaged.

The healthcare industry needs change, and nurse managers cannot sit back and think it's going to get better without getting personally involved. It's easy to say, "I'm too busy; I really can't take on one more thing." I know that is a true statement, but change needs your participation. Please take a stand and act now.

Nurse managers need to get involved with other nurse managers. It's hard to see different solutions if the only input you receive is from one organization, one field of nursing and one unit. Nurse managers need to share ideas, even if they seem weird. It's for sure the "sane" ones aren't working.

Compliance issues are big, but how important will they appear if we have no staff to implement them?

When we graduated from nursing school, we carried a lighted lamp to represent Florence Nightingale. Florence was a pioneer, and she helped establish the nursing field. Like it or not, it is our turn to help establish the professionalism of nursing.

As leaders in our industry, if we stand together and work together, we can make a difference. We can redevelop communication lines among each other and perhaps put a halt to hiring the same bad apple over and over. We must stop being held prisoner by poor workers.

Nurse managers need to be proactive. If we get out and help lay groundwork for the future, we can be ready for tomorrow. Join professional groups and learn how to write congressmen, senators and even the President. Ask them to help change the image of healthcare. Give these representatives ideas on how they could better represent us. With their help and a change in our image, we may be able to recruit quality individuals.

Visit colleges and volunteer to speak to nursing students. Introduce these students to your chosen field of nursing. There are many types of specialties in nursing, and each is rewarding. "Wine and dine" nursing teachers. Ask these teachers to take a look at where the care industry is headed. Ask for their help. Demonstrate the changes that are taking place in healthcare, and show nurses that hospitals are not the only places graduate nurses can develop technical skills. Today's transitional units are what hospitals used to call medical care units a few years ago.

Approach high school counselors and volunteer to have a student interested in healthcare shadow you for a day or a week.

Improvement starts with action. I am not advocating that nurse managers take up a lamp like Florence Nightingale, but it would be nice if each one would agree to help make a difference. Local nurse's groups are a great place to find other leaders wanting their voices to be heard. If there is no such group in your area, then start one.

Grab a flashlight and hold it up so other nurse managers can see that they aren't alone and that you agree that patients and residents are worth standing up for. Hold that light up high and, without a doubt, you will see a *light at the end of the tunnel.*

"If they speak not according to this word, it is because there is no light in them." —Isaiah 8 v 30

CHAPTER 10

My Roots Are Showing!

*"To know from where you come is a glorious
gift that some easily take for granted!"*

MAMA

Mama, a gentle lady, who knew no strangers.

Eager to please.

Caregiver and sharer.

Daddy, her reason for living.

Her daughters, her greatest success.

She loved being a military wife. Moving was not an inconvenience; it was an adventure. She was born in the South, yet she was destined to see the world.

The lady with the cute southern accent learned to speak Italian and Chinese, but her love for others surpassed the need for the spoken word.

Mama made friends no matter where she lived, from the California coast to the Delaware Bay, from the north of Alaska to the south of Italy. All the way to the far east of Taiwan, people knew my mama by name.

If you placed Mama in a desert, she would start a conversation with a camel; if you put her on a deserted island, she would have the lizards talking. Need your hair cut, curled or permed? Mama was your lady! Don't worry about the expense, because a smile and a friendly conversation were her only charge.

I remember as a child saying, "Mama, can't we just go to the store and come right home? Do you have to talk to everyone?" or "For heaven's sake, Mama, do you have to do everybody's hair on base?"

What I would give now to be able to take a trip to the store with Mama and wait while she shared with everybody or to sit across the kitchen table and watch her cut hair!

This wonderful lady taught me to:

- ✓ Love God
- ✓ Never be rude to others
- ✓ Share with those less fortunate

- ✓ Behave as nice as you look

    and, most important,

- ✓ Always make time for your husband

She will not be traveling the world anymore or cutting the neighbor's hair or even fixing a meal for her husband, for her memory is lost to Alzheimer's! But for as long as Mama is alive, she will be making friends and leaving her imprint on the hearts of all who surround her and care for her.

I love you, Mama, and as long as I am capable, I will remember and share all the great things you did for others and me.

"A mother is the truest friend we have, when trials heavy and sudden fall upon us; when adversity takes the place of prosperity; when friends desert us; when trouble thickens around us, still will she cling to us, and endeavor by her kind precepts and counsels to dissipate the clouds of darkness, and cause peace to return to our hearts." —*Washington Irving*

DAD

A man always on a mission, he was born in Pennsylvania, but he lived his life around the world. He was a handsome man, you could never find a wrinkled item on him, and he was ever so proud to be a military man.

As a young man, Dad could dance the night away and still rise early to jump out of an aircraft. He went to South Carolina, he thought, to learn how to fly military gliders, but to his surprise he found "his mate for life": a Southern belle for whom, he claims, he had to buy her first pair of shoes to take her across the Mason Dixon Line.

World War II was in full bloom, but Dad and his Southern belle married and, in the midst of all the gloom, their love gave birth to a beautiful redheaded girl.

One day, his military commander called and, without hesitation or question, Dad left his comfortable home to fight for world peace. With a kiss and a gift of another child, Dad was off to Europe. He returned a solemn and tortured man.

For the next 30 years, alcohol became his battlefield. Joy was fleeting and happiness hard to grasp, but finally his determination won out and reversed the tables. His last 24 years were alcohol-free and full of memories worth recalling.

He was forever a giving man. If you asked for a nickel, he gave you a quarter. His home was a refuge for many a family member. With hardly enough money to pay his own bills, he would never say "no" to a soul in need.

Around the world he went with his family in tow, developing strengths in his girls that would benefit them both later! This was especially true for one particularly stubborn, green-eyed, brown-haired, talkative daughter: His wisdom guided her with tools that later enabled her to lead an "army" of her own.

On July 16, 1997, Dad found his panacea. He no longer is searching for the next assignment. A faithful husband, a good father, a good provider and a friend for life!

He gave his best, and now his Father is giving him his best.

I love you, Dad. Rest in peace.

- Your baby girl

"Dad, your guiding hand on my shoulder and your memories in my heart make my every day better."

My next adventure is but a dream away. Adventure is in my roots. I traveled the globe with my dad, and my husband has moved me to 10 different states during our marriage. I risked when I established Tobin & Associates and it worked well, so I will risk again and again. Life is nothing but an adventure.

I will keep moving forward until I can't remember why I'm doing what I'm doing; then I pray that one of my children or grandchildren will step in and continue the legacy. I once stated in an interview, "As long as you are breathing, you should be dreaming." I'm still breathing, so I'm still dreaming!

A Third Generation of Caring

by Nic Tobin (grandson)

I grew up in a family of healthcare workers. I used to watch my family respond at all times of the day, evening and night, when the phone rang and a need caused them to stop all their personal activities and readjust their focus.

One Christmas Eve, we had just finished opening our gifts and were teasing one another when the phone rang. The message was that water pipes at the care facility had frozen and burst, and the resident hallways had ankle-deep standing water. Without hesitation, our family sprang into action. All of those who were old enough to help piled into the car to go to the facility.

My dad made the event a fun activity. We sang while we mopped water. It wasn't too long before a resident poked her head out of her room and said, "I just want you two boys to know I can't swim." We just had to laugh. Even though this was a comical comment and the possibility of drowning was nonexistent, my dad asked me to go into the other resident's rooms to reassure them – touch them on the hand or arm and let them know they were going to be fine and that I loved them. I was excited to visit and comfort my friends!

Around 5:30 a.m., the water leaks were plugged, the hallways were dry, and things were generally under control. As I walked down the hallway, I looked into the residents' rooms. The majority of the individuals appeared to be sleeping or resting well. Even though our family Christmas time together had been interrupted – and even though all of us were tired and sleepy – not one of us complained. We just smiled at one another and said, "What's next?"

I think this might have been the first time in my eight years that I understood what caring really meant. By age 10, I was volunteering in a nursing facility.

Gone are the days when my mom, dad and grandparents were involved in the daily operations of a nursing center, but now, at the age of 23, I remain involved! If I were asked why, I would probably say, "It's in our family's blood."

I have a 19-year-old sister who is a nursing assistant in a long-term-care facility. She plans to start nursing school in a year. My 18-year-old sister works in the dietary department of a different facility as a server. We represent a not-too-uncommon "third generation of caring."

We care and stay involved in long-term care because the generation before us showed us that:

- You reap rewards by giving without expecting anything in return.
- If you think of it as a job, you won't survive.
- The doing will come easy when you take the time to understand.

I'm glad to be in long-term care, even though, as my sisters and I agree, the work can be challenging. My nursing assistant sister says the success of her shift depends greatly on her attitude: When she makes up her mind to be positive, it impacts everyone around her!

My sisters and I are lucky to have a family of caregivers to turn to for support and advice. The changes that are occurring in the facilities are overwhelming but positive. The residents like being given choices; this type of patient-centered care appeals to me because I know that I don't like being told what to do all the time either.

Quality to me is a personal measurement. One resident or patient may consider someone's putting a throw over their feet excellent care, but to another, the same action could be seen as an invasion of their privacy. Only personal interaction lets you know the difference.

In any healthcare setting, success comes when the people who choose caregiving at any level and in any setting learn that building relationships is the most important service we will ever deliver:

Quality cannot be achieved without caring - Caring does come at a price, however ... perhaps in the form of giving up a Christmas Eve at home with your family opening presents.

Before I close, I want to share 10 effective leadership tools you might want to keep close to you on your journey to success:

#1. Roll of Tape

God gave us two ears and one mouth for a reason. We are to <u>listen</u> more than we are to talk. Keep a roll of tape in your toolbox to remind you to keep quiet and listen beyond the words.

#2. Squeak Oil

Keep this handy to <u>reduce</u> the squeakers who insist on being heard when they have nothing to say and only sound like a "squeaky wheel."

#3. Wrench

You want to remain <u>flexible</u> and able to adjust to changes. A wrench can open wide to handle big issues yet easily adjust to accommodate smaller ones.

#4. Butterfly Net

Don't forget to run after your <u>dreams</u>.
Catch them and then dream again!

#5. Shoes in Many Styles and Sizes

You want to <u>walk</u> in your associates' shoes before you judge them. Take the time to get to know them and their uniqueness.

#6. A Jar of Honey

Make your <u>words</u> sweet… just in case you have to eat them later.

#7. A Slice of Humble Pie

To help you never forget that it takes a <u>team</u> to succeed
and that "Pride cometh before a fall."

#8. Liquid Eye Drops

Keep your leadership <u>vision</u> clear –
so real that you can taste it, smell it and touch it.

#9. A Stack of Thank You Cards

You can never say "thank you" enough times.

The next tool is the most important! Without it, you will <u>never</u> experience true success.

#10. Your Moral Compass

Enjoy life, and remember to write to those who helped shape you into the leader you are today. Let them know you appreciate what they did for you, and please be specific about what they did that impressed you so much that it made a lasting imprint on you. Make time for those in your life who bring you joy and happiness.

Reference Books:

Personality Plus: How to Understand Others by Understanding Yourself, by Florence Littauer 7.1.1992

Understanding How Others Misunderstand You (DiSC Profile), by Ron Braund and Ken Voges 7.1.1995

Working with Emotional Intelligence, by Daniel Goleman 1.4.2000

Good to Great: Why Some Companies Make the Leap and Others Don't, by Jim Collins 10.16.2001

Now, Discover Your Strengths, by Marcus Buckingham and Donald O. Clifton, Ph.D. 1.29.2001

Delegate or Suffocate, by Peg Tobin, RN 8.21.2012

Outrageous Love, Transforming Power, by Terry Wardle 2004

Useful Tips and Guidelines:

Interviewing for a Leadership Position

- Think differently about an interview and how it is more of an audition than a fact-finding mission.
- Show a strong level of interest in the position. Often employers hire the candidate they feel is the most interested in the opportunity.
- Be confident in your ability to do the job. A lack of confidence will be interpreted as a lack of enthusiasm and interest. Once this perception is formed, there is no way to change an employer's decision.
- Make the interviewer feel as if they can't live without you. Put everything on the table that you can do for them, remembering to praise the team behind you.
- Prepare ahead of time the reasons for leaving all past employers. Review and emphasize what you've learned. It's very important to keep these reasons positive.
- If you plan to discuss a job opportunity with family or friends, do this prior to the first interview.
- Don't ask about compensation, salary, time off or benefits on the first interview.
- Understand that the way you accept or decline an offer is the client's first impression of your decision-making process.
- Remember that your main mission is to accept a position you can develop in and contribute to the success of the whole.

Creating a Great Resume

Get noticed and showcase your talents!

Resume Layout

First and Last Name, Credentials

Complete Home Address

Home and Cell Numbers, Email

Objective

A resume's "Objective" statement lets an employer know which specific job or internship you are interested in. When applying for a position, you should customize it so it relates to the position for which you are applying.

Accomplishments and Attributes

- Strong Knowledge of Regulations' Scope and Severity
- Competent RAI Process MDS
- Strong Verbal and Written Communication Skills

Professional Experience

- For each position, specify:
    - ✓ Beginning and end dates, including month and year
    - ✓ Number of beds/size per building
- Stay away from the "typical job description" format
- Bullet point at least three of your ROIs (Returns on Investment) – for example, Survey Results, CMI, RUG Scores, Turnover, Budgets
- What makes you stand out?

- Why should this company hire YOU?
- Which of your accomplishments are you most proud of?
- What exactly have you excelled in?

Education, Certifications and Licensure
- Name of the school or university
- Years attended
- Degree attained

References
- Supply at least three names
- Identify at least one of each hierarchy – Subordinate, Peer and Superior – include First and Last Name, Credentials, Current Position, Hierarchy to You, Address (preferable), Phone, Email)

Do:
- Include financial improvements, census numbers, percentages and personnel numbers
- Keep resume to two pages (references can form a third page)
- Use clear and professional fonts (Times New Roman 11pt, Verdana 11pt, Arial 11pt, Tahoma 11pt, Garamond 12pt)

Do Not Include:
- Personal information
- Fabrications
- Salary history or salary requirements

Making Yourself a Marketable Leader When You Face These Obstacles

Unstable work history:

Companies will hire you, but they are not going to pay a recruitment firm a fee to do so. Nonetheless, stay in touch with a recruitment company, because later on you will want to use it to promote yourself. Once you secure a job, <u>stay there at least 18 months to two years</u>. This tenure will make it easier for you to be presented to sought-after organizations.

Limited wardrobe:

How you dress and present yourself will leave a lasting impression. Research the company and their dress code. You don't have to wear the most expensive items, but you do want them to be clean and pressed. Don't show up in a suit if the culture is for everyone to dress casual. However, muscle shirts, cut-offs and bare midriffs are not acceptable at this time for a first interview. First impressions are vital, and this investment will pay off. For both men and women, limit the jewelry and go lightly with the cologne/perfume.

Last employer won't give you a good reference:

Some employers may not be pleased that you left the company, and so will not give a strong reference. However, if you have stellar references from other sources, the one bad employer reference can be explained.

Gaps in your employment:

You need to have an explanation for all gaps. Keep explanations positive, and make sure you include exact dates for all your positions. It is advisable to work at temporary or contract assignments while you are seeking full-time employment. This action will continue to make you marketable!

Terminated from your last job:

This can be a difficult situation to overcome, but sometimes there is a valid explanation for the departure. Keep every reason for separation positive. Terminations do make it difficult for recruitment firms to assist you with your next career move, because clients pay a fee to identify top talent that is currently working. Consider accepting a temporary assignment, which many times can lead to a full-time position.

Freeze when tested:

Testing is becoming the norm, so you may want to practice taking tests at home by going to typingtest.com. With practice, you will be amazed how comfortable you can become with the testing process. People who freeze with testing have proven to be insecure and doubtful of their abilities. Become positive about who you are and what you have to offer, and you will find that tests will only solidify how good you are in reality.

Resume needs sprucing up:

Keep your resume to two pages, and highlight your talents and what you bring to the table in your desired position. Briefly outline your responsibilities (do *not* write a job description), and then, under each employer, include three bullet points highlighting your personal accomplishments. If you have ever saved an employer time or money, include details. Make sure your objective does not limit your ability to grow with the company. Proofread your resume several times, and ask trusted professionals to review it. Many resumes can get screened out due to simple errors.

Writing a Letter of Resignation

A resignation letter can help you maintain a positive relationship with your old employer while paving the way for you to move on. You never know when you may need a previous employer to give you a reference; therefore, it makes sense to take the time to write a polished and professional resignation letter.

Your resignation letter provides an <u>official notice</u> that you are terminating your employment with the company.

How to resign:

When you resign from your job, it's important to resign gracefully and professionally. Give your employer the required company notice, write a formal resignation letter and be prepared to be asked to leave on the same day you submit your resignation. Be resolved with your decision to resign prior to submitting your resignation.

What to include in your resignation letter:

A basic resignation letter should include the fact that you are resigning and the last day you will work. It is fine to thank the employer for the opportunities they have provided to you, as well. It is also OK *not* to say thank you.

Keep it brief. Your resignation letter should be brief and to the point. You don't need to include lengthy explanations about why you are resigning.

When to include a reason:

If you're resigning under positive circumstances – such as you are relocating or going back to school – it is fine to include the reason. If you are resigning because you are in a bad position, there is no need to mention the negative details. Venting solves no issues; it is best to remain dignified and quiet.

Offer to help. If it is feasible, the professional behavior would be to offer to help during the transition and a short period afterward. The offer might not be accepted, but it will demonstrate your professionalism. Include a phone number and email address where you can be contacted.

Don't quibble. Make it clear that you are not open to counteroffers. Use a clear-cut line, such as, "I hereby submit my resignation." It is customary for senior executives to give more than a two-week notice.

Do not vent. Even if you hate your job, don't say it. Your resignation letter will be placed in your permanent employment file, and it is important that it does not contain much more than the basics.

Writing email resignation letters:

It is better to resign in person and have your resignation letter with you rather than resigning in person and then following up with a formal resignation letter for your employment file. It is never professional to leave a resignation letter on your superior's desk along with your facility keys and no notification. If circumstances are such that you need to send a resignation email, write it as professionally as you would a resignation letter on paper.

Sample Resignation Letters

Date

Dear Mr./Ms. Last Name:

Please accept this letter as notification that I am leaving my position, Specify Title with Company Name, effective Month/Date. I appreciate the opportunities I have been given at Company Name as well as your professional guidance and support. I wish you and the company much success in the future.

I will wait to hear from you as to what to expect as far as my final work schedule, accrued vacation leave and my employee benefits. If I can be of assistance during this transition, please let me know.

Sincerely,

Your Signature

Your Typed Name

Date

Dear Mr./Ms. Last Name:

I would like to inform you that I am resigning from my position as Specify Title for Company, effective Month/Date. Thank you for the opportunities for professional and personal development that you have provided me during the last Number years. I have enjoyed working for this organization and I appreciate the support provided me during my tenure.

If I can be of any help during this transition, please let me know.

Sincerely,

Your Signature

Your Typed Name

Date

Dear Mr./Ms. Last Name:

I am writing to inform you of my decision to resign from my position as Specify Title with Company Name effective Month/Date. I appreciate the opportunities I had with Company Name, and all the contacts I have made. I wish the company all the best for the future. If I can be of any assistance during the transition, please let me know.

Sincerely yours,

Your Signature

Your Typed Name

Date

Dear Ms./Mr. Last Name:

I am writing to formally notify you that I am resigning my position as Specify Title with Company Name. My last day of employment will be Month Date, as per the requirements under the terms of my employment contract.

I appreciate the opportunities I have been given at Company Name and your professional guidance and support. I wish you and the company success in the future.

Yours sincerely,

Your Signature

Your Typed Name

Date

Dear Ms./Mr. Last Name:

I am writing to formally notify you that I am resigning my position as Specify Title with Company Name. My last day of employment will be Month Date, as per the requirements stated in the terms of my employment agreement.

I wish you and the company success in the future.

Sincerely,

Your Signature

Your Typed Name

Review of Are you Setting the Pace ...or taking up space?

Donna DeFranco - Colorful Language, LLC - Editor
As I read this, I just keep thinking how much I needed it eight years ago when I was a co-leader of the creative services department at the bank. These principles cross industries; they're certainly not limited to nursing. I picture managers going through this with a highlighter and dog-earing pages! You are going to improve corporate culture all over the place!

Reviews of Delegate or Suffocate

Diane Stewart, RN, LHNA
I read the book over the weekend. One of the things I really like about it is the down to earth language used. It's warm and friendly and sounds just like the author is talking to the reader. I think it is ideal for any leader not just nursing. I'm going to have to buy a case of them to give to new nurse managers.

Jackie Siegrist, Banking Management
This book is Fabulous!
• Easy to read
• Fun and keeps your interest
• Pictures are so appropriate
• I love the quotes throughout and the ones below the pictures.
Nurse managers only? No way... anyone can use the insight! Applicable to any management job. The personal situations that were shared helped me to relate and apply to my own circumstances. So glad I bought it.

Mary Taylor, Attorney/LNHA/RN
What a GREAT book! What every manager needs to know! Even seasoned managers will benefit from the authors wisdom! FABULOUS and INSPIRING !!!
I will be buying a supply to share with the managers in my region.

Grace Roller, RN, BA - Kax'eil ti - SEARHC - Mt. Edgecumbe Hospital
Our management team rose to the top by default for the most part. We needed help so I went looking for tools to use. I found very few books written about nursing management on a personal basis. I read a few pages and decided we had to have this book. In this book we found inspiration and someone we could relate to. This book made us re-think what we were doing and helped us formulate new directions.

Kathy Chapman – Ohio Health Care Associates
In 2012 we started passing out 'Delegate or Suffocate' at our Nursing Leaders Core of Knowledge Training and the feedback has remained the same; 'thank you… the book is easy to read and is extremely relatable'.

Made in the USA
Lexington, KY
03 December 2019